A Beginner's Guide

ONEWORLD BEGINNER'S GUIDES combine an original, inventive, and engaging approach with expert analysis on subjects ranging from art and history to religion and politics, and everything in between. Innovative and affordable, books in the series are perfect for anyone curious about the way the world works and the big ideas of our time.

anarchism	forensic science
aquinas	french revolution
artificial intelligence	history of science
the beat generation	humanism
biodiversity	islamic philosophy
bioterror & biowarfare	journalism
the brain	lacan
the buddha	life in the universe
censorship	literary theory
christianity	machiavelli
civil liberties	mafia & organized crime
classical music	magic
cloning	marx
cold war	medieval philosophy
conservation	middle east
crimes against humanity	NATO
criminal psychology	oil
critical thinking	the palestine–israeli conflict
daoism	philosophy of mind
democracy	philosophy of religion
dyslexia	philosophy of science
energy	postmodernism
engineering	psychology
the enlightenment	quantum physics
evolution	the qur'an
evolutionary psychology	racism
existentialism	renaissance art
fair trade	the small arms trade
feminism	sufism

Magic
A Beginner's Guide

Robert Ralley

ONEWORLD

OXFORD

A Oneworld Paperback Original

Published by Oneworld Publications 2010

Copyright © Robert Ralley 2010

The moral right of Robert Ralley to be identified as the
Author of this work has been asserted by him in accordance with the
Copyright, Designs and Patents Act 1988

ISBN 978–1–85168–713–8

Typeset by Jayvee, Trivandrum, India
Cover design by vaguelymemorable.com
Printed and bound by CPI Cox & Wyman, Reading, RG1 8EX

Oneworld Publications
UK: 185 Banbury Road, Oxford, OX2 7AR, England
USA: 38 Greene Street, 4th Floor, New York, NY 10013, USA
www.oneworld-publications.com

Contents

Acknowledgements   vi

Illustrations   vii

Introduction: Magic and the magi   viii

1   **A pact with Hell**   1

2   **Harnessing nature's hidden powers**   32

3   **Tricks and illusions**   64

4   **The occult**   94

5   **Analysing magic**   130

Epilogue: Magic today   160

Further reading   165

Index   168

Acknowledgements

Thanks are due to several people: my editor, Marsha Filion, and an anonymous reader, both of whom provided invaluable criticism; Lauren Kassell and Sheila Nolan, for discussions and advice; and Jill Whitelock, to whom I owe a particular debt of gratitude for her indefatigable help and forbearance. None is responsible for any of the book's remaining flaws.

Illustrations

1 These shapes and characters form several of the
   ars notoria's theology *notae* in a thirteenth-century
   version from British Library MS Sloane 1712, f. 21v
   © The British Library Board. Sloane 1712. All rights
   reserved.   22

2 Some of the items with which John Dee practised
   magic © The Trustees of the British Museum   50

3 The equipment for the 'Decollation of John the
   Baptist', from Scot's *Discouerie of Witchcraft* (1584)
   Reproduced by permission of the Syndics of Cambridge
   University Library   74

4 Éliphas Lévi's image of the 'goat of Mendes', or
   Baphomet, supposedly worshipped by the Knights
   Templar; from *Dogme et rituel de la haute magie* (1855)
   Reproduced by permission of the Syndics of
   Cambridge University Library   102

5 The cabbalistic 'Tree of Life', from Athanasius
   Kircher's *Oedipus Aegyptiacus* (1652–4)
   Reproduced by permission of the Syndics of
   Cambridge University Library   113

Introduction: Magic and the magi

Magic was an accusation long before it was a practice. Today we might associate it with deception and illusion, perhaps with charlatanry; unusual power, exercised in secret; we might think of spells and incantations, to gain advantage or cause damage. It is sometimes used to describe the beliefs of people from distant cultures. Many of the magic-related stereotypes we harbour are negative: witches and sorcerers are typically portrayed as evil. All of these notions can be traced directly back to the classical world. To the ancient Greeks, who coined the word, magic was an umbrella term for a number of fearsome and dangerous practices familiar from legend and myth: enchantment; sorcery; witchcraft; deception. These were connected by the suspicion that they were all pursuits of the mysterious Persian magi, the visitors from the east at the biblical nativity. Magic was what they thought the magi did. It was only later in antiquity that a small group of Greek philosophers depicted magic as a positive and worshipful activity. They opposed the widespread fear and condemnation, and embraced magic as genuine wisdom about the natural world.

Such disagreements are at the heart of the history of magic. No definition of magic, no interpretation or analysis of it, has ever been uncontroversial. Nor have the questions of what counts as magic and what does not, or who is practising magic and who is not. Magic, in short, is hard to pin down. All of which can cause problems for anyone trying to discuss it in broad terms. This book is guided by its subjects: it includes those who claimed to be practising magic and who advocated it; it includes accusations of magic (however unfounded) and the people who made them. It is a book about debates around magic, as much as it is about practices. What magic was, what it involved and who was doing it were questions that people wrangled over for centuries. In order to understand magic – to appreciate where it came from, and how it comes to occupy its place in modern culture – we need to pay close attention to the answers that they came up with. With that in mind, this introduction begins in the ancient world, exploring classical views of magic and the prejudices and beliefs that shaped them. These provided the foundations for all later discussions of magic. Magic, for these early writers, was intimately connected to the magi, so the next few pages also trace their changing portrayals by writers from ancient times through the Christian tradition to the modern period. These attitudes have shifted in parallel with the magical tradition, and clearly demonstrate the importance of ancient debates to the history of magic.

Before magic (Greek *mageia*, Latin *magia*) there were sorcerers, enchanters and witches. Sorcery (*goeteia*) seems to have been a well-established concept by the time Plato characterized it in the fourth century BC. In his account, sorcerers created illusions and cast spells to constrain the wills of unwitting subjects. Alongside the sorcerer stood the *pharmakis* (or *venefica* in Latin), perhaps best translated as 'witch'. This was someone who used substances to harm people, either by administering them directly (as drugs or poisons) or at a distance (in a charm, for instance, perhaps accompanied by an incantation). Romans suspected witches of malicious acts such as moving neighbours' grain to their own fields, or casting charms over neighbours' fruit; these deeds were specified in the earliest law codes as punishable by execution. Later laws singled out for comment those who attempted 'anything against the life or person of anyone' or who were 'found guilty of influencing chaste minds to lust'.

Soothsayers or prophets (*harioli*) were just as dangerous and should not be consulted. The law likewise forbade summoning the spirits of the dead or sacrificing to devils (*daemones*). By that time (the fourth or fifth centuries BC) any of these activities might be considered magical. Magic, for the Greeks and Romans, was about raising the dead and dealing with spirits; it involved deceiving and hurting people, by casting spells, using charms, administering poisons. Its practitioners might claim healing powers but they were not to be trusted. Perhaps the first clear description of 'magic' as a field of activity was by Pliny the Elder (AD 23–79); convinced of its 'utter falsity', Pliny described it as a seductive blend of medicine, religion and astrology. In short, 'magic' was chiefly an accusation (not to say an insult): it was something one attributed to others.

Yet from around Pliny's time, some began to think of magic as a good thing – a positive activity that had simply acquired a bad reputation. Philo of Alexandria (20 BC–AD 50), a Jewish writer heavily influenced by Plato, was one of several philoso-phers who redeployed the word as a badge of honour. The 'true magical art', he wrote, was 'a science of discernment, which beholds the books of nature with a more acute and distinct perception than usual'. There was nevertheless one (fake) type of magic practised by charlatans who convinced clients that they could cause love and hate and hurt people through charms and incantations – in short, the magic traditionally feared. Later followers of Plato agreed that magic was an important way of engaging with the natural world; the hugely influential scholar Plotinus (AD 205–70) referred, like Philo, to a 'true magic', which was performed by harnessing nature's hidden powers and virtues. For these men magic could be good.

If there was disagreement over what activities constituted magic, it was clear what the word *meant*: literally it referred to the activities of the magi (in Greek, *magoi*), who came from Persia. The association between these men and the practices labelled magic (whatever they might be) was spurious but well attested. Pliny, dismissing magic, wrote that the art had 'originated in Persia, under Zoroaster'. Philo, supporting it, noted that no one could be king of the Persians without being initiated into 'the mysteries of the *magoi*'– by which he meant magical wisdom. In fact, we have no evidence that the magi practised anything that we might recognize as 'magic' at all. The magi were members of an ancient Persian caste or tribe (sources are unclear) who conducted important rituals. We know from the Athenian author Xenophon (*c*.430–*c*.355 BC) that they sang 'hymns to the gods at daybreak' and sacrificed to them daily. Herodotus (*c*.480–425 BC) reported that a *maguš* (the Greek *magos* borrows directly from the Persian) was 'always present at sacrifices' to pronounce incantations recounting the birth of the gods. Those gods, he noted, included the sun and moon, earth, fire, water and the winds. Persian sources confirm the importance of the magi in sacrificial rites, as well as their administrative function within the royal court.

At some stage they shifted to Zoroastrianism. Derived from the complex and intricate teachings of the ancient sage Zarathuštra, this (in the simplified form that they seem to have known) had a good spirit battling an evil one for control of the world, with good behaviour tipping the balance one way and evil behaviour pushing the other. The magi officiated at Zoroastrian fire ceremonies.

Ancient attitudes towards these men and their practices were at best mixed. Cicero described them as 'wise and learned among the Persians', but Tacitus called the arts 'absurdities' and Heraclitus denounced the rituals of these impious 'night-wanderers'.

Today they are more familiar as the travellers from the East visiting the infant Christ in St Matthew's Gospel. King Herod, having seen a portentous star, seeks their wisdom on its significance; told that it signals a child's birth, he sends them to

Bethlehem to find the baby and bring back word so that (in the familiar words of the King James version) 'I may come and worship him also'. Led by the star, they find the nativity scene:

> when they came into the house, they saw the young child with Mary his mother, and fell down, and worshipped him: and when they had opened their treasures, they presented unto him gifts; gold, and frankincense, and myrrh. And being warned of God in a dream that they should not return to Herod, they departed into their own country another way.

It is curious to note that there is no evidence that the magi interpreted omens or dreams (though Herodotus suggested that they did); nor do Persian sources give much basis for believing that they had any astronomical or astrological interests. In fact, as used by many Greeks, the term *magos* could refer to the priests of any Eastern cult: for all the world of difference between a Persian *maguš* chanting incantations over sacrifices, and a Babylonian *Kaldu* (Chaldaean) observing the stars, they were equally likely to be called *magoi* by the xenophobic Greeks. The Romans made just as little distinction. The fourth-century Christian writer Calcidius described the magi as 'the wisest of the Chaldaeans'. It is therefore possible that the men called *magoi* in the New Testament are Chaldaeans themselves.

Contemporary views of the gospel story tended to avoid the issue of what the magi's expertise was, instead emphasizing the men's foreignness and piety. Where the issue could not be avoided, commentators denounced them. Origen (*c.*AD 185–254) wrote that the magi had consorted with demons, relying on spiritual powers that they had lost when Christ was born. Alerted by this, the magi had gone to pay homage to the child. Justin Martyr (*c.*AD 100–65) described the Gospel story as showing the magi 'turning from superstition to the adoration of the true God'. Ignatius of Antioch (*c.*AD 35–107), reading the

Gospel perhaps only a generation after its composition, explained that by the star 'all magic was dissolved, and ... ignorance was removed'. Augustine (AD 354–430) argued that the heavenly omen was 'new and unprecedented', beyond the magi's experience and knowledge, and that they must have been told what its meaning was by angels. Presented with this revelation they had visited Christ, implicitly renouncing their prior beliefs. Returning to the same subject years later he explained that the star had 'confounded the futile calculations and divinations of the astrologers, when it pointed out to star-worshippers the creator of heaven and earth as the proper object of worship'. While such a view seems to have been almost unanimous in the early and medieval church, there are occasional glimpses of other interpretations. John Chrysostom (c.AD 347–c.407), who believed that by making the star appear God had been indulging pagan superstition, noted with some irritation that certain Christians were using the story to demonstrate that astrology was trustworthy. The degree of care necessary when discussing the magi's role in the nativity was presumably heightened by the presence in the Acts of the Apostles of two other figures, Simon and Elymas, who were each referred to as 'magos' and whose roles were unequivocally unsympathetic. An additional account in the apocryphal Acts of Peter described Simon Magus levitating to convince a crowd that he was a god, only to fall to the ground when the apostle Peter prayed for God's help. Lying on the ground, his legs broken, he was stoned to death by the angry mob.

Medieval accounts of the magi typically depicted them as kings. Psalm 72 had referred to kings bringing tribute and paying homage to the Messiah, while Isaiah 60:3 was thought to predict that kings would walk in the light of the star heralding his birth. So the visiting magi, previously men of obscure and dubious learning, must be kings. Not only did this mean the fulfilment of prophecy, it also provided an implicit blessing of royal power – important from Constantine's time onwards, when Christianity changed from a marginal cult of little influence to a key part of the institutions of state. Occasionally there were hints that other views of the magi survived, particularly in the common medieval belief that carrying a piece of parchment bearing their (legendary) names would prevent epileptic seizures. There were further stirrings of a reassessment of their knowledge. Roger Bacon (c.1214–c.1292), an English Franciscan and philosopher who was eventually imprisoned for his unorthodox views, claimed that God had 'willed to arrange his affairs in such a way as to show rational souls by means of the planets certain things which he foresaw or predestined'. The magi (whom he called 'philosophers') had been guided astrologically to the nativity, 'led solely by the impulse of reason'.

Despite official opposition, this focus on the magi and their wisdom became increasingly attractive during the Renaissance. Petrarch (1304–74) considered Zoroaster the inventor of the magical arts. Marsilio Ficino (1433–99), a cleric and scholar, emphasized the magical wisdom and astrological abilities of the magi. For him, their position in St Matthew's Gospel suggested that pagan learning generally, and magic in particular, could be a path to Christian faith. He explained that divine wisdom had been bestowed on Zoroaster before Christ's birth, and that Zoroaster had passed this wisdom down via a tradition that included the Egyptian sage Hermes Trismegistus (Hermes the Thrice Great), Orpheus, Pythagoras, and Plato.

Now that the magi's wisdom was increasingly emphasized, the very words in which the biblical account was presented to its readers were altered. The King James Bible calls the *magoi* who visited Jesus 'wise men', while Simon and Elymas, the *magoi* encountered in the Acts of the Apostles, are 'sorcerers'. Few if any English language Bibles since then have rendered the word the same way in both places.

This shift towards depicting the magi as 'wise men' reflected the fact that the importance of magic to the story was once more being effaced; the magi, by the Enlightenment, had come to represent secular learning. When Voltaire complained that everywhere 'the feast of the Kings is celebrated, nowhere that of the Magi', it was their role as representatives of (non-scriptural) wisdom that prompted the thought, not their reputation for engaging in magic. The emergence of occultism as a movement during the nineteenth century, however, brought with it a resurgence of interest in magic's history, and the *magoi* were incorporated into a broader account of the development of magical doctrines and practices. According to one history of magic, the magi were 'the adepts of Magic': 'we may even call them the priests of the wisdom of antiquity', it added. They were

> philosophers dedicated to the study of the universe, that sphere whose centre, they said, is everywhere, whose circumference has no bounds, and at the heart of which are united without being confounded – or are separate, without being lost from sight – the physical, the intellectual and the divine worlds: the triple face of all knowledge, the triple base of all analysis, the triple stem of all synthesis.

The *magoi* in this account were precursors of the modern occultist: privy to mystical knowledge, in tune with the world around them and espousing through their magic something akin to a religion.

This has remained an unusual attitude. At various times, the magi have been depicted as wise men or kings, knowledgeable and powerful or fearful and superstitious; magic has been championed as spiritual or rational, astrological or mundane. For most people it remained as mysterious (and perhaps as frightening) as it had originally been to the ancient Greeks. The ongoing conflicts between the proponents of these different views are the backdrop for the rest of this book. Chapter 1 returns to the Christian tradition, tracing official views of magic from the classical world in which Christianity first took hold, through the theological debates of the Middle Ages, to the mysterious world of the necromancers and the witch trials. Chapter 2 charts the rise of natural magic, magic as a way of gaining power over the physical world. Renaissance writers proposed grand cosmological systems in which magic played a central role, while contemporaries employed magical techniques in the service of everything from medicine to spiritual enlightenment, via the search for stolen goods. Chapter 3 addresses the theme of magic as spectacle and deception, from courtly displays and street conjurors to the stage magic that took hold during the Enlightenment, and modern illusionism. Today, stage magicians are some of the most vocal rationalists. Chapter 4 takes up the story of modern occultism and the re-emergence of magic as counterculture. Chapter 5 confronts the issue of rationality: in the nineteenth century, anthropologists studying other cultures used the word 'magic' as a technical term that positioned it somewhere between religion and science. Much of the historical work on the European magical traditions has been guided by the work of these scholars. The book closes with an epilogue that discusses where this leaves us: magic as performance, magic as ritual practice, magic as a sort of ritual hinterland between religion and rationality. What is magic today?

I start, however, by returning to the classical attitudes to magic and its practitioners. The earliest Christian writers were products of those traditions, and their teachings would guide the history of magic for two thousand years.

1

A pact with Hell

For Christians, magic has always involved the devil. Early Christians feared the same bundle of assorted myths and beliefs as classical writers, but what linked them now was not magi but demons. Magic still involved binding people's wills, cursing them, calling on spirits, raising storms; damaging and harming. The crucial difference was the belief that these things could only be done with the help of the devil and his servants. Those who successfully cursed others (for instance) must have demons working for them. Anyone who worshipped a non-Christian god was practising magic. Most worryingly, it was entirely possible to be relying on demonic aid and not realize it. Sometimes magic was the action of Satan's representatives on earth; sometimes it was a way of trapping the unwary, curious or greedy. Either way it was devilish. However old the word 'magic' might be, and whatever classical precedents there were, it was specifically this formulation that has shaped attitudes ever since. This chapter looks at how classical views of magic were turned into this Christian doctrine. It shows how missionaries reinvented pagan charms and amulets for the Christian world, and how divination became demonic. Ancient necromancers had consulted the dead; their medieval successors consorted with devils. Meanwhile theologians debated what demons could do, and what counted as magic. Witches had once been seen as simply malicious – by the end of the Middle Ages they were Satanic. The chapter ends with the Reformation debates in which Catholics and Protestants accused one another of magic and devil-worship.

Early Christianity: inherited and new views of magic

Christian authorities, taking over the remnants of the Roman Empire from the fourth century AD onwards, inherited the classical notion of magic: a jumble of harmful and unpleasant practices supposedly linked to the Persian magi. They saw these men as outsiders, subversives, perhaps charlatans. It was easy to find examples in the Bible; early Christian writers had these caricatures in mind when they wrote of the magi who had visited the nativity, or Simon Magus and Elymas, who are described in the Acts of the Apostles as using magic to turn

TWO ANCIENT LATIN CURSES

Archaeologists have discovered a large number of lead tablets bearing inscribed curses that were buried – or rather, sunk, as they tend to be found in watery sites such as wells and springs – in antiquity. They are often folded or rolled up and sometimes transfixed with nails; the texts use the Latin word *defigo*, 'I fix' or 'fasten down', to describe what is to be done to the victim, and as a result the word came to mean 'bewitch' or 'curse'. One example from the ancient city of Nomentum, near Rome, contains two curses – one on each side. The first reads: 'Malchio son of Nico: eyes, hands, fingers, arms, nails, hair, head, feet, thigh, stomach, buttocks, navel, chest, breasts, neck, mouth, cheeks, teeth, lips, chin, eyes, forehead, eyebrows, shoulders, upper arm, sinews, bones, marrow, stomach, cock, leg, business, money, health, I curse in this document.' On the reverse side it says: 'Rufa the public slave: hands, teeth, eyes, arms, stomach, breasts, chest, bones, marrow, stomach ... [words missing] ... legs, mouth, feet, forehead, nails, fingers, stomach, navel, c—t, womb of this Rufa Publica I curse in this document.' Such fierce imprecations have been unearthed across the Roman Empire.

people against the faith (both are called 'magoi'). They read the Old Testament account of Pharaoh's servants using incantations to match the miracles performed by Moses. Here again, magic was an evil imitation of divine miracle.

In Christian doctrine, magic could only be effective if it involved demons. 'Demons' (Greek: *daimones*; Latin: *daemones*) already had a long history in various forms: to Romans and Greeks they were neutral spirits, lower than the gods but higher than humans and free to do good or ill. In ancient Greece they might be lesser gods or ghosts of the dead. Centuries ago, Hesiod had written that the men of the world's Golden Age had been changed into *daimones* by Zeus to act as guardians to mortals. People secured the help and protection of a *daimon* by paying respects at its shrine. According to Plato, Socrates had claimed to be aided by a small *daimon* that warned him of mistakes, and the later Greek rulers (from Alexander the Great on) were believed to have guiding *daimones*. By late antiquity, Greek and Roman gods were increasingly seen as distant from the affairs of the world, impassive and motionless; *daimones* remained on earth, subject to the same physical and spiritual forces as people. There were good *eudaimones* who watched over people, and evil *kakodaimones* who deceived and caused harm.

Christian writers, in contrast, made all demons evil. They were fallen angels. One third-century treatise explained that they were 'impure and wandering spirits' that sought people's ruin. They hid in statues and supposedly sacred images; they interfered with the motion of birds, fire, spilled entrails – anything used by seers to predict the future; they deceived people by mixing truth and falsehoods, and caused diseases which they could then appear to cure. One of the early Church's most influential authors, St Augustine of Hippo (AD 354–430), wrote that demons had invented magic and taught it to people, and that it was those same demons that actually carried out what practitioners wanted. Even in the cases of apparently innocent natural phenomena, such as the ability of certain rocks to attract iron, demons might be involved: if spirits were not directly participating, they might still have provided guidance and instruction. In one way or another, magic implied demons. When the archbishop and encyclopaedist Isidore of Seville (c.AD 560–636) rehearsed the familiar list of arts that constituted magic, he included many forms of divination, plus enchantment (the magical use of words) and ligatures (binding magical items to someone to cure an illness). 'All such things involve the art of demons', he claimed. Magic was demonic, and consulting demons was magic.

Non-Christian religions were also magical, as their false gods must be demons. This attitude was a classical survival: in the ancient world, the term *mageia* had often been used as a convenient way of abusing others' religious practices. Ancient Greece's civic elites had called the religion of rural outsiders 'magic', though they were no less likely to lay curses on people (an activity that contemporaries clearly defined as magic). The distinction between religious activity and 'magic' had never been totally clear: magical practices sometimes involved appealing for divine aid. The magical papyri of Roman Egypt invoked higher gods such as Helios, to gain power over the *daemones* whose help was needed. Further north, Germanic mythology associated the god Woden (Odin) with the runic alphabet and held that he could use its magical powers to accomplish wonderful things; his aid is often requested in charms that have survived.

Many classical writers had reckoned that religion became magic when it was carried out in secret, for evil ends. (Some modern anthropologists have agreed: see chapter 5 on this.) Christians painted the issue with broader strokes. Christianity was religion, anything else was magic. A verbal formula seeking the aid of the Christian deity was probably a prayer; if it mentioned some other divinity then it was a spell, addressed to a demon. As with Moses and the Pharaoh, any wondrous deed performed by a Christian in God's name was a miracle, but any performed in the name of some other religion was magic. Again, Simon Magus was a key example: the Acts of the Apostles depicted him fooling the inhabitants of Samaria into believing that his magical powers were actually divine. These men were dangerous imposters, conspiring with demons; they were to be rooted out.

As magic's definition shifted from secret, maleficent religion to non-Christian ritual (and to consorting with demons), so the legal strictures surrounding it changed. Roman laws had prosecuted people who harmed others; who stole crops, raised storms, called up the dead. How they did any of these things was a secondary issue. Later amendments forbidding love magic, divination, and healing magic received little attention. After the emperors' conversion to Christianity, magic itself was made an offence – regardless of intent or effect. From AD 357, those in the empire caught engaging in magic or divination were to be beheaded. Ammianus Marcellinus (c.AD 330–398), a pagan writer, complained of the fierceness of the new laws, pointing out that anyone who sought help from a soothsayer, or used 'some old wife's charm' to ease an ache, could legally be executed. Magic involved demons, was reprehensible, and was now explicitly banned.

Nevertheless, pagan attitudes persisted; of particular importance to the later history of magic was a school of philosophers in late antiquity who followed Plato's teachings – later called the 'Neoplatonists'. These men developed a philosophical religion which centred on practices they considered magical. The first of the Neoplatonists was Plotinus (c.AD 205–70), who wrote that magic and prayer both worked by harnessing the cosmos's natural links and hidden sympathies: in fact, he claimed, 'every action has magic as its source'. In other words, the way in which spells and prayers worked was natural – but obscure. Prayer to gods or to heavenly bodies had an automatic effect, just as plucking one end of a string on a musical instrument would make the other end move too. Magic could be used to attack people, but it could also be used to defend: by developing the mind's higher powers of contemplation, Plotinus claimed, it was possible to guard against magical offensives. They might still cause disease or suffering, but the victim's true self would be unscathed. Plotinus' student and biographer Porphyry (c.AD 233–304) reported that Plotinus had indeed rebounded one spell back onto its originator.

Porphyry's student Iamblichus (d. c.AD 330) focused on 'theurgy', which involved rites for men to commune with gods. Porphyry and successive other critics rejected these rituals as coercive and therefore magical rather than properly religious: one should not presume to order the gods around. Iamblichus disagreed: a theurgic invocation, he wrote, 'makes the intelligence of men fit to participate in the gods, elevates it to the gods, and harmonizes it with them'. Theurgy brought men to the level of gods. Its exponents saw themselves as being in harmony with the gods and with cosmic sympathies; they contrasted theurgy with sorcery (*goeteia*), whose practitioners drew on those same natural sympathies to more nefarious ends. As distant as all of this was from orthodox Christianity, the positioning of magic was exactly parallel: Neoplatonists distinguished between (good) religious practice and (evil) sorcery. Few in ancient and medieval Europe believed that magic was a positive activity, few saw themselves as practising it. For the most part magic remained a slur rather than a practice.

Charms, amulets, and talismans

Many of the activities that ancient writers considered magical involved using magical objects, writings, and charms. They believed that certain items had powers that might protect, heal, or harm. There is little consistency in the terminology used, but we can loosely characterize three groups: amulets (whose power derived from their substance), charms (which involved magic words, as invocations or inscriptions), and talismans (where characters and figures were inscribed on objects, such as rings or stones). Amulets were made from stones, plants, or animal parts, materials often explicitly linked to magic – by critics if not by exponents. In a few lines on gems in Pliny's *Natural History*, for instance, we find a claim attributed to Zoroaster that a precious stone called 'astriotes' was useful for the 'magical arts', alongside Pliny's own note that a particular form of another stone, a variety of 'ceraunia' only found on the site of lightning strikes, was 'sought after for the studies of the *magoi*'.

Charms, in contrast, were often simply written down. 'Ananizapta' was one example, deployed in charms against various medical complaints and problems. A protective charm recorded by Reginald Scot in the sixteenth century went (in the English translation he provided):

Ananizapta smiteth death,
whiles harme intendeth he,
This word Ananizapta say,
and death shall captiue be,
Ananizapta ô of God,
haue mercie now on me.

Where writing or symbols were engraved onto an object, the result was a talisman. One perhaps surprising example of this type was the coin: made from metal and bearing the ruler's image, coins were considered powerful items and were often used as amulets. John Chrysostom, the Archbishop of Constantinople, complained in the fourth century AD about people 'who bind bronze coins of Alexander of Macedon around their heads and feet', and considerable archaeological evidence attests to the wearing of coins throughout late antiquity. Christians regarded these practices with considerable suspicion. Verbal formulas that appealed to pagan gods were clearly in veneration of demons, as were the observances and rites demanded when preparing certain charms, while the makers of naturally effective amulets might have begun under demonic instruction. In the eyes of the early Christians, all of this was certainly superstitious (involved a misuse or abuse of religion) and was probably magical.

In response, Christian missionaries (often monks) produced Christian versions of pagan charms, replacing the names of pagan

---

ABRACADABRA

One magic word in particular has become famous since its use in charms: 'abracadabra'. It was employed in the Mediterranean region from ancient times, and is mentioned as late as 1722 by Daniel Defoe in *A Journal of the Plague Year*. The word was written out repeatedly, each time removing a letter, to form an inverted pyramid:

```
A B R A C A D A B R A
A B R A C A D A B R
A B R A C A D A B
A B R A C A D A
A B R A C A D
A B R A C A
A B R A C
A B R A
A B R
A B
A
```

The paper on which it was written would be rolled up and worn round the neck. Other magical words, some much longer, were used in the same way.

gods with those of Christ and the saints. To guarantee effectiveness, the user would accompany these either with rituals and observances (such as fasting) or with peculiarly Christian symbols, such as the cross or (for instance) images of the nails from Christ's crucifixion. The resulting charms resembled prayers, blessings, or exorcisms and, whatever the theological niceties of using them to heal or protect, they were more recognizably Christian than their predecessors. This solution did not satisfy everyone; St Augustine warned that those 'who seduce through amulets, through spells, and through the machinations of the enemy, may mingle the name of Christ in their spells'. According to this hard-line view, the simple Christianization of charms was not enough to make them acceptable; that said, nor was Augustine's opposition sufficient to curtail their use. In the surviving books that list charms, the word 'magic' is seldom used.

By the later Middle Ages, charms routinely referred to Christ, saints, relics, and the other paraphernalia of Christian devotion. One common example found across Europe claimed that it was possible to avoid sudden death, illness, or tribulation by evil spirits (among other unpleasant experiences) by looking at or carrying a one-fifteenth scale illustration of Christ's body. Another made similar claims for someone who bore a measure of the length of the nails used on the cross: Pope Innocent VIII, one Middle English version implausibly claimed, had granted gifts such as invulnerability to poison or sword and the certainty of an honest living to whoever carried this and 'worshipith devoutly the iij naylis' by saying daily the Lord's Prayer five times, five Hail Marys, and the Creed. Some charms employed Christian names and terms within unfamiliar formulas. The Dominican John Bromyard (d. c.1352) criticized one that went: 'Holy Mary enchanted her Son from the bite of elves and the bite of men, and joined mouth to mouth, blood to blood and joint to joint, and so the child recovered.' If historians sometimes think they detect in such formulations the remnants of pagan practices, there were some surprisingly physical survivals from pre-Christian times. One charm, bestowed as a gift by Charles V in the mid-fourteenth century, was originally Roman and dated back to the first century AD. A cameo made from agate, this had Jupiter, crowned with laurel, holding a thunderbolt and leaning on a lance with an eagle at his feet. By 1367, when Charles gave it to Chartres Cathedral, the figure was taken to be St John the Evangelist, and around that time two inscriptions were added, reading (in Latin): 'But Jesus passing through the midst of them' (a reference to Luke 4:30), and the opening of John's Gospel, 'In the beginning was the word'. The first of these was believed to guard against dangers during travel, the second to ward off demons and protect against lightning.

During this period, works composed in or translated into Latin confronted the issue of astrological talismans, items believed to attract astral influences. In one sense, using these was simply the other side of astrology: those people who understood what effects the heavens had on earth could use those effects to their own purposes. The celestial bodies (especially the planets) ruled over particular substances and images, and by manipulating the substances and images those bodies' powers could be harnessed.

One of the most notorious of the magical works circulating in late medieval Europe was an Arabic manual of astral magic known to the West as *Picatrix*, translated from Arabic to Spanish in the thirteenth century and subsequently reproduced in Latin. It provided a manual of magical techniques, a catalogue of examples by which assorted ends could be achieved, from creating love between enemies or enmity between friends, to razing cities to the ground. Where images were to be drawn it specified what the image was and what it was to be drawn on; it explained the conditions under which the process was to be carried out. Lastly, it described what to do with the item afterwards – was it to be 'suffumigated' with a particular kind of smoke (the various substances were listed), or buried in a certain place, or burned? Worn on the person? *Picatrix* advocated prayer to the planets and provided forms of words to employ: a typical prayer would involve invocation by name (in different languages), praising the planet for its powers and seeking help.

Other works containing similar guidelines passed quietly through the hands of scholars across medieval Europe. One translator defended the spreading of the information on the grounds that it was a tool provided by God for the furtherance of good and the punishment of his enemies. Theologians and inquisitors were unlikely to be convinced. Though explicit mentions of demons were comparatively rare, the fundamental appeal of such magic to demonic aid was clear to orthodox readers. The possessors of magic books such as *Picatrix* were persecuted by Church authorities from at least the fourteenth century.

This, however, was only the most extreme (and learned) talismanic magic in medieval Europe. Far more people used those charms drawn up by monks during earlier centuries, or established by lay use, and probably did not consider them magical. By and large they drew on biblical and Christian names and tropes, they resembled or even copied official rites and practices (such as prayer and exorcism), and they provided (for example) a way of responding to illness. To many churchmen they were superstitious, involving a misplaced religious fervour, but only magical in certain cases. Identifying these cases occupied some of the continent's most respected thinkers.

Theological debates

Such recognizably magical activities as the use of charms were widespread in medieval Europe, and Augustine had insisted that all magic involved demonic aid. As a result, it was important for medieval theologians to decide what people should and should not be allowed to do. Two of medieval Europe's greatest philosophers and theologians, the Dominicans Albert the Great (*c.*1200–80) and St. Thomas Aquinas (*c.*1225–74) agreed with Augustine on the centrality of demons to magical practice: Albert explained that this was 'the common opinion of all persons'. They nevertheless labelled as non-magical many other activities that seemed equally suspect. To the truly suspicious, of course, little was entirely free of the risk of demonic involvement: it was even possible that healers whose remedies were strictly herbal had been instructed by devils. A great deal of thought went on in the medieval period into the issue of what kinds of action or speech were permissible.

Telling the difference, for instance, between the prayers at the heart of Christian worship and the spells and charms to be guarded against, was not always easy. The clearest cut cases were the obviously illicit spells or conjurations that were addressed to beings other than God. Nonetheless, books of astral magic and necromancy sometimes referred to their verbal formulas as 'prayers'. These were clearly forbidden. There were, however, borderline cases in which prayers or parts of prayers were employed in charms (either spoken or written), and used in combination with rites and observances. These examples were more excusable but still exasperated theologians. In the fourteenth century John Bromyard explained that any efficacy in prayers was down to the moral worth of the person praying – not the precise way of setting them down or carrying them, and certainly not the addition of stories or magical phrases. In general, while amulets were probably safe provided they only drew on the natural powers of the cosmos, as soon as symbols or characters were added (as in a charm or talisman) the result was dangerous. The standard church line held that written inscriptions must be attempts to communicate with intelligent entities

– which, as angels did not stoop to such matters, must invariably mean demons.

Some arguably magical activities, such as the production of charms, were often criticized not as magical but as 'superstitious': this made them a misunderstanding rather than a malicious crime. A superstitious person overestimated the power wielded through particular words, objects, or acts. Texts from the Bible were the most familiar battleground. As we have seen, setting down a verse and carrying it was an extremely common way of warding off illness and other mishaps, but this (as a fifteenth-century manual of witchcraft explained) was to place too much emphasis on the words and the process of writing, and not enough on their meaning and God's intention behind them. Although the words themselves were holy, their use was sinful. So went the official line, though users often presumed otherwise.

The issue of astral influences exercised many theologians trying to assess where magic stopped and nature began. Aquinas, like his teacher Albert the Great, believed that stars could influence the body, which in turn could influence the soul. Aquinas argued that most people were ruled by their bodily passions, few having the intellect and will necessary to overcome these. Therefore the stars freely influenced the majority of the population. The will was still, in principle, free, and anyone wise enough (and sufficiently strong-willed) could fight and evade this influence.

Aquinas also explained that in the cases of such phenomena as the attraction of iron by magnetic rocks, or the purgative powers of rhubarb, these powers were impressed upon the items by the heavenly bodies – which were also responsible for the formation of minerals and the growth of plants. On the other hand Nicole Oresme (c.1325–82), a French philosopher and theologian, denied the stars any terrestrial influence except the provision of heat and light, and reckoned that magicians pretended (perhaps even to delude themselves) that they were operating using stellar powers when in fact their actions were illicit and probably ultimately demonic.

While Aquinas was willing to accept that the stars ruled over much that happened on earth, he was less convinced by the suggestion that their powers could help (for instance) in the recovery of stolen property. Practitioners claimed that they could divine the perpetrator of a theft or make an inanimate object speak by purely natural means; Aquinas argued that these activities must involve the aid of a rational agent. Since much magic of this sort was carried out to nefarious ends, those beings must surely be demons. His logic reflected an active suspicion common among churchmen. The Chancellor of the University of Paris Jean Gerson (1363–1429) denounced a physician for relying on the curative properties of a medal inscribed with the image of a lion and some characters.

Considerable discussion went on about the question of how much power the soul had over the physical world. Some theologians from the thirteenth century onwards were willing to accept that the evil eye might well be a natural phenomenon, and (drawing on Arabic sources) suggested that this was down to the soul's power over bodies other than its own. It was widely accepted that the imagination of a pregnant (or conceiving) woman could affect the appearance of her baby. One second-century writer reported that the 'tyrant of the Cyprians who was misshapen, compelled his wife to look at beautiful statues during intercourse and became a father of well-shaped children'. So was it not possible that that same imagination could affect external objects or people? Roger Bacon claimed that women with double pupils were capable of killing simply by looking, and that some people corrupted in body and soul were able to cause evil through thought alone. Sometimes it was the imagination that was thought to be affected by some external cause: Oresme proposed that the words used in incantations might have some physical impact on the imagination of a person hearing them, which would in turn affect that person's body. The imagination was central to many theories of how magic might work.

It was precisely the way in which the spirit related to the physical world that was at issue in discussions of magic. We are familiar with the notion of a 'supernatural' realm distinct from the natural world, but strictly speaking this was God's province alone. Supernatural acts were divine acts. The devil and all angels and demons occupied an intermediate position between these two extremes: the 'preternatural'. They lay outside nature but not above it. The devil could not perform miracles, entirely unnatural events; demons could not create things or change them from one substance to another. Any magic which made it appear that they had done so was illusory. What demons could do was harness natural processes, manipulating or even accelerating them to achieve impressive feats. Miracles were not within the reach of the devil, but wonders and prodigies were; the biblical episode in which Moses faced the Pharaoh's magicians was frequently used to demonstrate the superiority of divine miracles over devilish magic. For similar reasons, demons did not actually know the future: only God was privy to that. Instead, according to Augustine, they predicted it by conjecture based on experience and intelligence, with the intention of ensnaring diviners.

This ensnarement was the reason for demons' involvement in magic. Even when those dealing with demons believed themselves to be in control, according to orthodox theologians, they were being duped. The thirteenth-century physician and theologian Arnald of Villanova rejected the idea that people could coerce demons, either by themselves or with the use of natural objects, because demons were entirely incorporeal and so not subject to anything made of matter or linked to matter – whether gemstone, herb, or human mind. Throughout the Middle Ages, theologians agreed that evil spirits were not bound by magicians but worked to trick them. Demons provided men with secrets, instructed them in the hidden powers of the natural world, aided them in carrying out their wishes and performing their spells; and they did so in order to trick magicians into turning away from God. Magicians might do things that would endanger others, but the chief risk was to their own souls. Even in cases where there was no explicit pact, a demon might well be involved without the practitioner's knowledge. Discussions of what items or actions were allowable were as important to practitioners as to the authorities.

Divination

Diviners in the ancient world told the future by reading natural signs. They observed the flights and cries of birds (augury); they inspected the entrails of sacrificed animals (haruspicy), and they plotted the positions of the stars and planets (astrology). Of these, astrology far outlasted the others. Although grand, mathematical, systematic astrology of the kind practised by Ptolemy (second century AD) was rare in Europe until the twelfth century, there was always interest in the movements of the moon and the other major heavenly bodies. Aside from these, there were other types of divination (in Greek, *manteia*, -mancy): Isidore of Seville picked out for scorn divination by inspecting earth (geomancy), water (hydromancy), air (aeromancy), and fire (pyromancy). Geomancy was the most popular of these from the medieval period onwards. To these lists might also be added the interpretation of dreams (oneiromancy), popular in the early modern era and beyond, with rules for interpretation ranging from the absolutely literal to the deeply complex; reading people's futures in their hands (chiromancy), or in calculations based on their names, turning the letters into numbers (onomancy); divination using reflective surfaces such as mirrors or crystal balls (catoptromancy). These examples could be multiplied; despite the best efforts of the Church authorities, and much to their disgust, diviners of all kinds remained at court and throughout society into the high Middle Ages and beyond.

Divination by means of the spirits of the dead (necromancy) was a classical staple; in Homer's *Odyssey* Odysseus is instructed by the sorceress Circe (who has turned his companions into swine) in the art of calling up the shades of the dead. He summons them to a trough filled with sheep's blood for them to drink and has them tell him the future. The biblical tradition had its own examples, most famously the witch of Endor: the first book of Samuel recounts her conjuration of Samuel's ghost at the request of King Saul.

Christians, however, refused to believe that souls could come back in this way, arguing that it must actually be a demon pretending to be the dead person. Necromancy, in Christian theology, was demonic magic, and the word itself even changed to accommodate this revision; by the late Middle Ages the term was often written as 'nigromancy', relating to the Latin 'niger' meaning black – almost literally 'black magic'. Necromancers, in this later tradition, were clerics trying to force evil spirits to serve them. Necromancy actually took place; far from being an invention of theologians or Church authorities, it was a combination of elements from the Islamic tradition of astral magic reflected in the *Picatrix* with Christian exorcism perhaps influenced by Jewish traditions. Medieval necromancy handbooks survive to the modern day, giving detailed instructions on the procedures to be followed.

Divination remained a central goal of necromancy: the manuals indicate how to force demons to reveal hidden knowledge of events in the future – or even the past or present (such as identifying a thief and locating the stolen item, or checking on someone away on a long journey). Spirits were believed to

CONJURING DEMONS

A conjuration taken from Cambridge University Library MS Dd.11.45 explains how to make an image that will allow you to destroy anyone you want:

> Image of Mars: make this from copper and red wax in the hour of Mars, and the names of the angels who order it to be done are as follows: Saliciel, Ycaachel, Harmanel; and the name of the devil king who commands is the Red Fighter, and his three helpers are these: Karmal, Yobial, Yfasue. Say this conjuration over the image: 'I conjure you, scribes of angels, who are flying through the ether: Aynos, Gaidis, Scadexos, Ames, Habes, Hayoynois, Mahamtas, Haiaras. Speed O you Samatiel, O you Casiel, O you Hermanel; by the name Bethahamar and however many, Arnanis and Elcus and Eudelmus, and there is another who has a pleasing name. Speed Lataleoleas and Prolege, Capaton, and by one king who rules the stars and the earth, and there is none besides him, and he is great and he is the most high. Speed O you Salatiel, O you Taxae, and you Harnariel, I set over the Red King and over his helpers!'

provide this information, appearing to a 'scryer': a virgin, usually a boy, who would peer into a crystal ball, a mirror, or even his own fingernail to discern the spirit there. Sometimes, if the question involved identifying someone – for instance, a thief – that person would appear instead. It was also possible, in a distant nod to necromancy's origins, to have demons animate the bodies of the dead to make them appear alive again. Necromancy was no longer simply a divinatory procedure, however; the spirits commanded were believed to be able to perform other tasks: they were supposedly capable of deceiving the senses, creating illusory banquets or a horse that would seem to carry the necromancer; they could aid in constraining the will of third parties, whether to love or hate, or simply to look favourably upon someone (often the necromancer himself). On rare occasions necromantic experiments were listed in handbooks as harmful or deadly.

Traces of ancient divinatory techniques are evident in the means by which necromancers worked. A contemporary Church inquisitor reports the burning of birds and animals, fumigating with incense and aromatic herbs, and throwing salt into fire – all recognizable as the practices of classical diviners. Whatever their roots, they were now procedures to summon and command spirits. By examining handbooks of necromantic 'experiments' (as they were called) we can get a clearer picture of the procedures involved. Practitioners drew out diagrams – the infamous 'magic circles' – on the ground using a blade or on parchment or cloth. These could be simple or complex, and involved words, characters, and symbols, sometimes with places marked for magical objects to go during the ritual, and a space set out for the necromancer himself to occupy. The necromancer would chant a conjuration, a command ('Coniuro te', 'I conjure you') for a demon or demons to perform some task, usually accompanied by elements of Christian prayer or liturgy. He would also carry out a physical act at the same time, whether sacrificing an animal, offering up some other substance (anything from ashes to milk), or performing image magic (manipulating dolls made to represent the people to be affected by the demons). Often there was also an incantation to be spoken that explained the actions. Necromancers were advised by their handbooks to ensure ritual purity before engaging in any experiments: to fast, to bathe, to be dressed in white, to be chaste for a certain number of days; this was primarily to help protect the necromancer from the evil spirits he would conjure, though Church authorities were more likely to see it as a way of showing reverence towards the demons. The procedures described look very like those of the imported astral magic of *Picatrix*.

The late medieval Church repeatedly demonstrated its fear of necromancy. Pope John XXII (1249–1334) drove a string of prosecutions for the crime in the early years of the fourteenth century. Best known is the case in 1317 in which he had the bishop of Cahors executed for plotting to kill him by manipulating magical images, but this was only one of a number of cases in which he intervened. In 1318 he established a commission to investigate necromancy and geomancy by several clerics at the papal court, in 1319 he had a French priest, a Carmelite friar, and a woman prosecuted for summoning demons by incantations and images, and in 1320 he demanded that the seneschal of Carcassonne hand over a priest and accomplices charged with sorcery – though he took no action when in the same year a Milanese cleric arrived at his Avignon court claiming to have been asked to take part in a magical plot to kill him. In 1323 John was overseeing the case of a monk involved in necromancy and sorcery with wax images. 1326 saw him instructing a cardinal to judge the case of a canon who was accused of summoning evil spirits to kill people through hail and thunderstorms, and who had magical books and vessels containing mysterious powders and liquids. Two accomplices had been caught having removed an arm and two heads from criminals on the gallows; one (a layman) was burned at the stake before the pope's involvement. In the same year the pope appointed a commission of three cardinals to judge three clerks and a prior charged with image magic and invoking demons. Five years later Philip VI of France complained that an abbot, a Dominican friar, and others were practising sorcery against him; the pope asked the bishop of Paris to deal with them.

John's successor, Pope Benedict XII (d. 1342), was involved in further cases: he had people accused of sorcery sent to him from Béarn, and an English necromancer from Paris together with some lead plates used in his magic. Faced with this veritable epidemic of sorcery and necromancy, John issued a decree in which he condemned practitioners of magic. These people, the text went, 'enter an alliance with death and make a pact with Hell, for they sacrifice to demons, adore them, make or cause to be made images, or a ring, a mirror, or a phial, or something else in order thereby to bind demons magically. They ask things of them and receive responses from them, and demand their help in achieving their depraved desires.' The penalty would be excommunication and possibly death. Necromancy was demonic magic, it genuinely existed, and it was a threat to the health and security of medieval Christendom.

One particular type of ceremonial magic, involving angels or demons according to one's point of view, outlasted straight-forward necromancy and survived until at least the seventeenth century: the *ars notoria* (notary art). This tradition, visible in Europe from the twelfth or thirteenth century, was usually linked with Solomon after the biblical account in which God bestowed on him wisdom and great learning. For months the practitioner prepared (by fasting, for instance, and consecrating the place) and regularly said prayers that included words and names that (texts claimed) were derived from Greek, Hebrew, Chaldean, and Arabic; the result was to be gifts of knowledge from angels and the Holy Spirit. Those who engaged in the art did so for improved memory, or perhaps access to university learning without the painstaking long-term effort of study. The 'notes' (*notae*) of the *ars notoria* were images that blended words and shapes relevant to the subject area with the divine and angelic names and prayers (see figure 1 for example). The practitioner inspected and contemplated these while reciting the relevant prayers. This visual dimension in particular exercised theologians, who denounced it vehemently as idolatrous; with its mysterious words and consecrations it also resembled necromancy too closely for orthodox tastes. Nonetheless, it survives in dozens of manuscripts from the period.

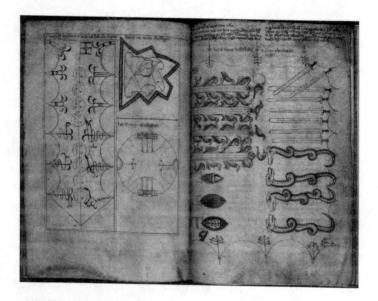

Figure 1 These shapes and characters form several of the *ars notoria*'s theology *notae* in a thirteenth-century version

Witchcraft

Towards the end of the Middle Ages the focus of inquisitors' ire shifted from necromancers to witches. The figure of the witch had long been a target of suspicion – the notion of witchcraft predated even that of magic itself, being one of the constituent ingredients of *mageia* as characterized in the ancient world. In ancient Greece, *pharmakeia* involved causing harm by potions or incantations, or providing substances that could heal or poison, and is closely related to the root of the modern word 'pharmacy'. A *pharmakis* might be sought out for medical help, but these women were presumed to have wider expertise. Ancient literature is replete with witches, from Circe, turning

Odysseus's companions into swine (a story accepted as historical truth for much of the Middle Ages), to the description by Lucan of the foul Erictho killing (and eating) babies and playing with corpses.

Into and through most of the Middle Ages, the Christian view of witchcraft (or *maleficium*, literally 'evil-doing') was that it concerned people harming others around them, prompted and aided by demons. It was believed that witches caused death and disease in people and animals; they bewitched men to make them impotent; they brewed storms to ruin crops; and they stole property, including honey or milk – which were thought to be transferred to the witch's own bees or cows. Most responses to this *maleficium* were distinctly unofficial. In 1074, rebellious burghers of Cologne cast one suspected witch from the town walls; in 1128 the people of Ghent disembowelled another. In 1279 monks saved a woman in Ruffach, Alsace, from being burned by peasants for sorcery. Official and ecclesiastical views of the witch tended instead towards contempt. In comparison with the real evil perpetrated by Satan and his demons, the practitioner's importance was slight, an error probably best corrected by penance. Genuinely demonic magic was discussed and condemned by such inquisitors as Bernard Gui (*c.*1261–1331) and Nicholas Eymeric (*c.*1320–99), but they were interested in it primarily as a form of heresy. Medieval witches were on the whole to be pitied rather than feared.

Early in the fifteenth century a new understanding of witchcraft emerged, probably based on confessions extracted under torture. From the 1420s a wave of trials gathered momentum, some presided over by the Holy Inquisition, others by bishops, and many by secular judges. As a result of them dozens and then hundreds of people were executed. We know of examples in Switzerland and France as early as 1428. These seem to have originated in prosecutions for heresy, a crime which, as described by contemporaries, had great similarities to witchcraft.

Both involved the participation of demons and a catalogue of unpleasant practices.

In part the concern with witches reflected long-held fears that the charms and spells, amulets and talismans, potions and powders to be found in use throughout medieval European society were demonically inspired and aided. Since the earliest years of Christianity, churchmen had claimed that devils lay behind many of the practices employed to divine the future, combat illness, and avoid misfortune. At the end of the Middle Ages this was pushed towards its most extreme conclusion: that large numbers of people were deliberately, rather than inadvertantly, engaged in satanic rites.

To their hunters, the witches of the fourteenth and fifteenth centuries were as blameworthy as necromancers: the devil did not hide and tempt in these cases – he was summoned. The new witch was an apostate: she had turned away from the true religion. She might still be a tool of the devil but she had exercised her free will by signing a pact with him and joining him as his servant. Witches' crimes now included the murder of babies (echoing the classical story of Erictho), both to satisfy their own desires and to harvest young flesh for use in their magical operations. Moreover, and crucially, witches were now conspiratorial. They were believed to meet at sabbats – or, as they were tellingly referred to before the mid-fifteenth century, 'synagogues'. They flew to these meetings and took part in parodies of the Eucharist and orgies, under the supervision of Satan himself (who appeared as a being half-man, half-goat). Witchcraft was endemic, widespread, and dangerous to the very fabric of Christian society.

Theologians began to compile books detailing this new view of witchcraft. One of the first to do this was the Dominican theologian and reformer Johannes Nider (c.1380–1438), who wrote at length on 'witches and their deceptions'. His account was hugely influential; it circulated in countless manuscript copies and was printed in seven different editions. It was also a source for the period's most (in)famous manual for witch-hunters, the *Malleus maleficarum* (*Hammer of Witches*, 1486). Both Nider's book and the *Malleus* presented the witch in her new form, dependent on demons to work her evil magic for her, murderously minded and inclined to feed on dead infants.

A WITCH CAUSES LEPROSY

The *Malleus maleficarum* reported a case from the diocese of Basel:

A labourer had spoken roughly to 'a certain quarrelsome woman', who responded by threatening revenge. That night he noticed a pustule on his neck and rubbed it, 'and found his whole face and neck puffed up and swollen', with 'a horrible form of leprosy' all over his body. The woman was captured and confessed. When asked by the judge how and why she had done it, she told him that when she had gone home incensed, 'an evil spirit' had asked her the reason for her mood. She had explained and pleaded for the spirit to get revenge; when asked how, she had replied: 'I want him always to have a swollen face.' The demon, however, had gone much further than she had anticipated, 'For I had not at all hoped that it would strike him with such leprosy'. Nonetheless, the woman was burned.

The witch trials continued through the seventeenth century. Under torture, those accused of witchcraft were pressured to denounce others in their community as co-conspirators, with the result that witch-trials tended to occur in groups. During the period of just over a century from 1561 to 1670, it has been calculated that at least 3,229 people were executed in south-west Germany alone. While this was going on, debate raged over the existence and activities of witches. The concept of witchcraft was well established through the vast swathes of written discussion in the burgeoning genre of demonology; whether or not it existed as it was usually understood was clear, as was how it might best be dealt with. All of these were considered at greater length than there is space to do justice to here. Those who denied the existence of witchcraft remained convinced of the existence of magic. Reginald Scot's *Discouerie of Witchcraft* (1584) claimed that many of the phenomena ascribed to demonic action were actually produced by natural magic. Nor did the shifts in the understanding of nature in this period drive a change in attitude: experimentalists such as Robert Boyle were as likely to believe in witchcraft as their scholastic Aristotelian predecessors. In fact, phenomena associated with witchcraft were among those that were to be collected, written out, and examined by members of the fledgling Royal Society of late seventeenth-century London. Nevertheless, during the seventeenth and eighteenth centuries, scholarly interest in witchcraft waned. Driven initially by judicial processes, intellectual debate seems to have subsided with them too.

Witch beliefs did not end with the trials, however. While the 'craze', the official purge, came and went, belief in witchcraft as straightforward *maleficium* seems to have continued outside the elites and authorities. It remained strong through the eighteenth and nineteenth centuries. A case reported in London in 1742 involved the assault of an old woman suspected of being a witch, in order to reverse a spell she had supposedly cast. Newspapers in the nineteenth century denounced as superstitious the perpetrators of similar crimes – as *The Times* did when reporting the assault of a claimed witch in Nottinghamshire in 1866. As late as 1895 Edward Burke of Gorleston in Norfolk was prompted by local rumour to place a notice in the *Yarmouth Independent* denying that his mother was guilty of 'sorcery and witchcraft, or that by the employment of some other person or persons did cause my wife to be laid on a bed of sickness'. When in 1928

accusing one another in terms that will by now be familiar: conspiring with the devil; practising magic, sorcery, witchcraft.

Protestants reserved most venom for criticizing the Catholic Mass, and specifically what Catholics believed was happening during the ceremony. Luther, Zwingli, and Calvin differed over what they thought *was* going on, but they agreed that the traditional account was untenable. Their objection was to the doctrine of 'transubstantiation', which held that the bread and wine offered in memory of Christ's body and blood actually turned *into* Christ's body and blood (though still looking, smelling, and tasting like bread and wine). This sounded to many Protestants like magic, and they described it in colourfully intemperate language. The sixteenth-century Tübingen theologian Jacob Heerbrand called Catholic rituals 'nothing but truly diabolical, ungodly, and magical blasphemies', while the seventeenth-century English philosopher Henry More wrote that Catholic priests claimed to have 'a power plainly Magical of changing the Elements in such a sort of all the Magicians of *Pharaoh* could never do'. This was compounded by their dislike of the obscurity of the Roman liturgy's language. Scripture and services should be in the vernacular, they argued, so that non-clerics could understand. Conducting ceremonies in Latin made the experience too reminiscent of performing spells: speaking mysterious (and perhaps incomprehensible) words in order to bring about some hidden but wonderful physical result. The Mass was so clearly magical to Protestant eyes that the English expression 'hocus pocus', first recorded in the early 1600s as the catchphrase of a stage magician, had by the end of the century been linked by the Archbishop of Canterbury, John Tillotson, to the Catholic Mass. Tillotson announced in a sermon of 1695 that the expression 'in all probability' was a corruption of the declaration 'Hoc est corpus meum' ('This is my body'). The truth of Tillotson's etymology may be doubtful, but the fact that so many people then and since have believed it gives us some indication of the resonance of these accusations among Protestants.

The Mass was not the only Catholic practice to arouse Protestant suspicion, however. Sacraments (ritual acts) and sacramentals (blessed items) were both derided by Luther, who denied that practical procedures and physical objects could produce spiritual results. Using water for baptism did not itself produce a spiritual cleansing; sacramentals such as the altar on which the Mass was conducted, or blessed bread, did not have the power to ward off evil. The spiritual realm acted continually in the physical world, but the physical world had no effect on the spiritual. Salvation was about accepting God's grace, not performing particular rites. As Calvin put it (in a contemporary translation), Catholics 'attribute vnto the sacraments magicall force, as if they did profite without faith'. Magic, to early modern Protestants, was a peculiarly Catholic mistake.

Their own societies were far from immune, however. Despite their hard line on sacraments and sacramentals, over several decades rituals, blessings, and the idea that certain items were 'holy' crept back into Protestant life. Protestant authorities stressed that none of these had any real power, but they were frequently ignored. Furthermore, where a problem demanded the use of a particular holy item that was unavailable, Protestant laity often simply turned to a Catholic priest to supply it. Protestant theologians concentrated their attention on what they considered the most pernicious magic in their societies, describing the faults that persisted. Magic rites sometimes involved evil words, as with the necromancers of old, directly invoking the devil; sometimes the words were harmless but were accompanied by superstitious acts, in a way which made them magical; often the words were misused passages from scripture. It was common for procedures such as medical cures to draw on the Bible or prayer books. John Bale (1495–1563), a churchman and controversial writer, complained of the way in which the Mass was used by 'witches in their witchery, all sorcerers, charmers, enchanters, dreamers, soothsayers, necromancers, conjurers, cross-diggers, devil-raisers, miracle-doers, dog-leeches, and bawds'. A report from Wiesbaden in Germany in 1594 bemoaned at length the locals' propensity to accompany with magic more or less any act or deal with any problem, 'in pangs of childbirth ... when cattle are driven into the fields, or are lost, etc., ... when someone feels sickly or a cow acts queer'. The name of God, the Holy Trinity, angels, the Virgin Mary, the twelve apostles, the saints, Christ's wounds, New Testament verses: these and others were 'spoken secretly or openly ... written on scraps of paper, swallowed or worn as charms' and accompanied by signs and gestures to bring luck or deal with a problem. Magic of this kind was arguably the hardest to stamp out because it appeared defensible; it remained to exercise Protestant theologians after the more obvious Catholic practices had long been stamped out.

Though accusations of magic are most characteristically Protestant, Catholics responded in a similar vein. They restated the traditional association between heresy and witchcraft: Simon Magus had been the first heretic, and heresy and magic were inseparable. Anyone not part of the true Church was consorting with demons. Protestants were heretics, so they must be involved in magic. At the turn of the seventeenth century the Jesuit Martin Del Rio claimed in his demonology that most of the recently confessed witches in Trier had blamed their 'infection' by demonism on the spread of Luther's ideas; Calvinism, he added, was causing similar damage in England, Scotland, France, and Flanders. The French writer Pierre Nodé linked witchcraft to the late medieval heresies of Jan Hus, John Wyclif, and Martin Luther and wrote of the prospect of an alliance between witches and the Huguenots; his fellow countryman Sebastien Michaëlis remarked that it was unsurprising that there was so little attention in Geneva to anti-witchcraft legislation as 'they have the property that all Hereticks naturally have, to love Magicians and Sorcerers'. The devil had caused these people to turn against the Church and placed them in league with his other followers.

In 1600, as in 600, 'magic' was a label that Christians used for religious practices they wanted to discourage. At various times it referred to the use of pagan gods' names to protect or heal, the summoning of spirits, and the Mass; pagans, necromancers, witches, heretics. The devil linked them all, tempting some into magic by providing charms to cure by strange words and symbols, pretending to do others' bidding so as to entrap them. Magic was the means by which the devil and his associates worked against Christian society, dividing, deceiving, and hurting people. From the late Middle Ages, however, another view of magic began to emerge: some saw it as a way of mastering and manipulating purely natural forces. Natural magic is the subject of the next chapter.

2
Harnessing nature's hidden powers

Renaissance magic was chiefly about power over nature. During the Middle Ages, to do magic had been to deal with demons; magic had been bad religion, practised by necromancers and combated by priests. In the Renaissance, while Church authorities held on to these views, a group of scholars dissented: their magic was about understanding the cosmos and learning to use the world's natural forces. It encompassed what we might now think of as folklore, science, technology, and astrology; and, alongside these, a few riskier activities – contacting spirits (not demons), interpreting texts 'mystically', and searching for spiritual enlightenment. It was practised by philosophers, who looked back to their classical predecessors and called themselves 'magi'. This chapter examines the rise and fall of the Renaissance magus. It begins with the earliest writers and their fascination with the influences of the heavens on earthly objects, and with the cabbala, which read mystical symbolism into the letters of the Hebrew alphabet. Renaissance magic was principally natural, but it provided a way to God. Meanwhile, the 'cunning men' (magical practitioners) of Renaissance Europe helped those who were ill, or who had lost something, or who wanted to know the fate of a loved one on a distant voyage, or find buried treasure. Members of the public consulted them but feared them, and they were portrayed in contemporary literature as evil or (at best) misguided. The chapter ends by discussing the claim that magic gave rise to modern science.

From natural magic to the divine

What European scholars achieved, over a generation either side of 1500, was a redefinition of magic. By that stage the idea that there was a non-demonic kind of magic was already perhaps two hundred years old. It would (its proponents claimed) achieve its aims not with the aid of evil spirits, but by using nature's hidden powers. While the great theologians had generally accepted that these mysterious forces in nature existed, they had tended not to use the word 'magic' to describe them. For Thomas Aquinas (whose opinions mattered more than almost anyone else's to medieval Christians), magic involved demons, and anything that did not involve demons was not magic. It might well be possible to cause wonderful effects by manipulating nature – but that was not magic. William of Auvergne (d. 1249), bishop of Paris, was one of the few who disagreed, clearly stating that there was a natural type of magic distinct and separate from the demonic version.

More outspoken was Giovanni Pico della Mirandola (1463–94), a young Italian nobleman of impetuous temper and prodigious learning. Pico looked back to the Neoplatonists of late antiquity (see chapter 1) and their insistence that magic was positive and was part of genuine religion. He reported that in Persian the word *maguš* meant 'interpreter and worshipper of divine things'. Magic was not only separable from demons, it was pious. It was also still about nature – which linked it to philosophy, rather than theology. Throughout the Middle Ages and up until the emergence of something recognizable as modern experimental science in later centuries, studying nature was what philosophers did. 'Natural philosophy' involved contemplating the natural world to understand it better. In 1486 Pico wrote that natural magic was 'the practical part of natural knowledge' and 'the most perfect achievement of natural philosophy'. It was the reason for doing natural philosophy. Sixty years later, a Neapolitan nobleman called Giambattista della Porta (1535–1615) divided magic into 'sorcery', which involved demons, and natural magic, which he called 'the most perfect knowledge of natural things'. Natural magic was 'nothing else but the survey of the whole course of Nature'. There was nothing, he added, 'more highly esteemed, or better thought of, by men of learning', than this. The 'Magician' was to be a skilled philosopher, physician, herbalist, distiller, mathematician (with knowledge of astrology), and know about 'Metals, Minerals Gems and Stones', and optics.

For Pico, magic was not only why one studied the natural world; it was also a way of worshipping God. In his view, a magus was a minister of nature and it was his divinely ordained role to govern the natural world. Natural magic, he insisted, led from contemplating the 'hidden wonders' of nature 'to the worship of God'. The whole universe had been corrupted by Adam and Eve's ejection from the Garden of Eden, because there was a correspondence between man (the 'microcosm', little universe) and the cosmos as a whole (the 'macrocosm', large universe); when Adam and Eve were made to suffer hardship and disease, the cosmos suffered too. The true magus should be able not only to better himself, improve his health and well-being, but to bring the rest of the cosmos with him when he did it. Magic was part of the plan for general salvation, engaging with nature for religious purposes.

One significant effect of the drive to make magic respectable was the rehabilitation of astral magic. In the Middle Ages, books on the topic such as *Picatrix* had been among the most infamous of banned texts. People who believed that the stars' influences could be manipulated and used tended not to refer to their activities as 'magic'. When such writers as Albertus Magnus and Pietro d'Abano (*c.*1250–*c.*1316), a Paduan professor of medicine, had discussed the use of talismans linked to the heavenly bodies, they had described it as part of astrology. In contrast, Pico was happy to count as magic the investigation of celestial and terrestrial powers (the effects of the planets, the virtues of plants, stones, animal products) and hidden links and sympathies (between planet and plant, for instance, or different kinds of stone).

A correspondent of Pico's was going still further in trying to establish a legitimate, Christian, natural version of astral magic. Marsilio Ficino (1433–99), a Florentine scholar translating Plato and the Neoplatonists into Latin for the Medici family, paused in his work to write one of the Renaissance's most influential treatises on magic. Entitled *De vita coelitus comparanda* (*On Obtaining Life from the Heavens*) it was completed and printed in 1489, three years after Pico's controversial statements. Ficino's view of the world was based largely on his familiar ancient texts – Plato and the Neoplatonists. God's Intellect had created things in the heavens, and these heavenly bodies then produced related items below on earth. That meant that below each planet there were numerous earthly things whose nature was derived from it and which it had influence over. The sun, for instance, had given rise to (and so ruled over) such stones, plants, and animals as gold, amber, saffron, cinnamon, the ram, the hawk, and the lion. The world, like people, had a body (the physical part that we encounter), a soul, and a spirit (a thin intermediate substance linking body and soul). Astral influences were propagated through the world spirit, which in turn affected the spirit in human bodies. Via the human spirit it could affect the human imagination, which was part of the soul. Astral magic was about managing astral influences to look after the body and soul of the individual.

Ficino's main interest was in how to use these influences for healing. He explained in his book that harnessing astral powers involved directing them to affect that particular person, and managing the person's spirit to receive them. Each planet could protect against a variety of illnesses, aid certain physical processes

FICINO ON ACQUIRING THE SUN'S BENEFITS

Marsilio Ficino in *De vita coelitus comparanda*:

If you wish your body and spirit to receive virtue out of some part of the world, namely out of the Sun, look for things which are especially Solar among metals and gems, among plants more, but among animals still more, most of all among people; for without doubt things more like you convey more. These are to be employed both outside and inside for the powers to be taken in, especially on the day and hour of the Sun and with the Sun ruling in the astrological chart. All gems and flowers which are called heliotropes are Solar, because they are turned to the Sun; so are gold and orpiment and golden colours, chrysolite, carbuncle, myrrh, frankincense, musk, amber, balsam, yellow honey, sweet flag, saffron, spikenard, cinnamon, aloes-wood, and the other spices; the ram, hawk, cock, swan, lion, beetle, crocodile, people who are blond, curly-haired, often bald, magnanimous. Some of the preceding things may be prepared as foods, others as ointments and suffumigations, still others according to need. These should be experienced and considered frequently and should particularly be loved; and plenty of light is to be sought.

and enhance characteristics; the magus obtained these 'gifts' by using substances and objects under the planet's power to prepare an ointment, food, or fumigation at an astrologically suitable time. The powers of stars and constellations were also available to those who performed pieces of music with the right harmonies or words. Songs could draw celestial influences down, and the human spirit up, allowing the two to meet in between. This could help cure an illness – or cause one, for that matter. Human imagination was as responsive to the right songs as it was to celestial forces. Moreover, a person's behaviour was enough to attract a particular influence: those who were given 'to gaiety and music and festivity' would come under the rule of Venus, for example. Probably the most useful guidelines that Ficino provided, however, were on preparing talismans. These were to be made by engraving astrological images onto suitable materials. Aquinas had distinguished between natural and demonic charms or talismans according to whether they had writing on them – if they required something with intelligence to read or understand a message, then they must be demonic (see chapter 1). Ficino reported all this but suggested that the engraved figures probably did little anyway other than through the warmth they generated in the surface during the process of inscription. Ficino's magic was reliant on strictly natural processes.

Pico, on the other hand, remained fascinated by the power of the written word. Though he wrote that magic worked by putting things together that were naturally separate, and exploring hidden sympathies of the natural world – in short, by exploiting and manipulating nature – he was at least as interested in the power of reading. One of the few aspects of magic that he discussed explicitly was the interpretation of texts; he noted above an explanation of one set of antique texts that his interpretation was 'according to magic, that is, the secret wisdom of divine and natural things first discovered in them by me'. Special techniques of interpretation enabled the wise reader to find secret messages. Magic, in this case, was about how to read things.

In particular, Pico appealed to the cabbala, Jewish mysticism based on interpreting Hebrew writings. While Aquinas had permitted images but denounced characters, Pico's sentiments were precisely the reverse. He wrote: 'We should not form images of the stars in metals' but went into great detail about the cabbala. Hebrew characters, he explained, 'have more power in an act of magic than any material quality'; he went so far as to claim that there could be 'no magical activity of any efficacy' without cabbala. The cabbala provided a way of understanding Hebrew text based on the hidden (often mystical) significance of particular letters. Much of Pico's cabbala involved the use of characters to invoke angelic powers; some of it was aimed at celestial bodies. Hebrew words not only represented parts of the cosmos, they were connected to it in some fundamental way that no other language could match.

It was not clear to everyone that cabbala was part of magic. Johann Reuchlin (1455–1522), a German courtier and scholar who met Pico in Italy in 1490, presented cabbala as an alternative to magic rather than the essential power behind it. Magic, for Reuchlin, was summoning spirits: if they were evil spirits it was *goetia*; if they were good spirits, it was theurgy. The dangers of being deceived and then damned by the machinations of a demon made magic of any sort too risky. Instead, Reuchlin wrote *De verbo mirifico* (*On the Wonder-making Word*), published in 1494, and *De arte cabbalistica* (*On the Cabbalistic Art*), 1517. *De verbo mirifico* was, as its title suggests, about using powerful words ('soliloquia') to perform wonderful deeds. Reuchlin accepted that there were hidden properties and powers in nature but steered away from discussing 'natural' magic in the book. Soliloquia involved using Hebrew, the language in which God had spoken with men and men with angels in Old Testament times; other languages (such as Greek) were corrupt, ineffective imitations. In Hebrew God had many names, each referring to a different aspect of his divinity; the most powerful was the Tetragrammaton (יהוה or YHWH). Each of its letters was symbolic: the initial *Yod* (י), for instance, had the numerical value 10, and represented undivided unity and the principle of extension, and signified the beginning and end of all things. Now, however (wrote Reuchlin), the powers of the Tetragrammaton had been transferred to the Pentagrammaton (יהשוה or YHSWH, which Reuchlin claimed was a Hebrew rendition of 'Jesus'). This name had brought the dead back to life, cured illness, and facilitated other miracles. It was to be used together with what Reuchlin called the secret word of the cross – which he did not disclose. Trying to command spirits was too dangerous, he contended; this provided a risk-free way of performing wondrous acts. Use the power of divine names and one's prayers would be granted.

Surveys and systems

The most enduring magical writings produced in the half-century after 1500 were surveys, based on the works of Pico, Ficino, and their contemporaries, and produced by writers who had known these men. The Renaissance magi visited and wrote to one another; Pico and Ficino corresponded for a number of years, while Reuchlin met Pico on a trip to Italy in 1490. Sometimes the details of these networks give fascinating hints that the circle of learned magi in this period extended beyond those whose works on magic have survived. In 1494, the year that his *De verbo mirifico* was published, Reuchlin travelled to Sponheim in the German lands to visit a former student who was now abbot of the Benedictine monastery there. Johannes Trithemius (1462–1516) had learned languages from Reuchlin, but he counted among his friends many of the period's principal magical writers, and claimed to have learned magic from someone called Libanius Gallus. Despite this we know of no work of Trithemius's that unequivocally concerns operative magic. What we do have are rather cryptic remarks along these lines: 'Study breeds knowledge, but knowledge produces love, love likeness, likeness community, community strength, strength worthiness, worthiness power, and power makes miracle. This is the only way to the end of magical perfections, divine as well as natural.' It is an intriguing comment, but hardly enough to reconstruct his world-view.

Two of the sixteenth century's most prominent writers on magic named him as their teacher: Heinrich Cornelius Agrippa von Nettesheim (1486–1535) and Theophrast Bombast von Hohenheim (1493–1541), a Swiss physician and mine worker known as 'Paracelsus'. Agrippa, an itinerant scholar, physician, and lawyer, presented Trithemius with the manuscript of his survey of magic *De occulta philosophia libri tres* (*Three Books of Occult Philosophy*) in 1510. Paracelsus (whose controversial ideas about medicine would cause uproar throughout Europe) claimed to have learned alchemy from the abbot. If these claims are true, they reveal an impressive legacy.

FRIENDLY PLANTS

From Agrippa's *Three Books* on 'the enmity and friendship' between things:

All things have a friendliness, and enmity among themselves, and every thing hath something that it fears & dreads, that is an enemy, and destructive to it; and on the contrary something that it rejoyceth, and delighteth in, and is strengthened by ... These dispositions ... are nothing else but certain inclinations of things of the one to another, desiring such, and such a thing if it be absent, and to move towards it, unless it be hindred, and to acquiess in it when it is obtained, shunning the contrary, and dreading the approach of it, and not resting in, or being contented with it ... [There is an inclination of friendship] betwixt the male palme and female: whereof when the bough of one shall touch the bough of the other, they fold themselves into mutual embraces, neither doth the female bring forth fruit without the male. And the Almond tree, when she is alone, is less fruitfull. The Vines love the Elme, and the Olive-tree, and the myrtle love one another: also the Olive-tree, and Fig tree.

Agrippa's *Three Books* was one of the Renaissance's most influential works on magic, guiding practitioners across Europe for at least the century after its publication, and arguably ever since. Laden with classical citations and demonstrating an impressive range of learning (in fact, his account was heavily indebted to Pico's and Ficino's), it presented a description of the cosmos and the magical powers within it. His interest in magical philosophy embraced several traditions and he drew them carefully together, dividing the cosmos into three and allocating a book to each region: 'elementary, celestial and intellectual'. In the first book he discussed what he called 'natural magic', the manipulation of things on earth to exploit nature's hidden links, sympathies, and antipathies: what could be done with stones, herbs, and animals, which planets influenced what items, and what kinds of terrestrial divination there were. Book 2 moved to the heavens, the realm of mathematics: from the virtue of numbers to the images of the stars, and the role of the 'Soul of the World'. Book 3 concerned the spiritual realm and ceremonial magic, providing theological details about God, discussing spirits and communication with them, explaining the mental states necessary for prophecy, and closing with an account of rites and observances. Each of these realms was higher than the last, and each book therefore described a higher wisdom and a more powerful type of magic, eventually reaching the divine. Later in the century, Agrippa's *Three Books* were supplemented by a fourth almost certainly not written by him, on 'magical ceremonies' (demonic magic): clearly illicit, this enjoyed a certain notoriety and circulation but scarcely on the scale of the *Three Books* themselves.

Agrippa's was not the only grand survey available to the discerning book-buyer. Giambattista della Porta's *Magia naturalis* (*Natural Magic*, first published 1558, then in expanded form 1559) provided similarly eclectic information under a multitude of headings. The twenty books that comprised the work covered topics such as 'the production of new plants', 'the Wonders of the Loadstone', 'Of perfuming', and 'Of tempering steel'. He discussed, among many other things, how to breed new types of animal, how to change one metal into another, and the secret of invisible writing. These were recipes and instructions to achieve particular ends or make certain substances. Like Agrippa he included the testimony of earlier writers and details of his own experiences; nonetheless, this was as far from the overarching philosophical systems and religious discussions of Ficino, Pico, and Agrippa as it was possible to get and still describe the subject as 'magic'.

THE WONDROUS PROPERTIES OF THE CROW

The Magick of Kirani, King of Persia (London, 1685) on the magical virtues of the crow:

> The Heart carried *creates Concord between a Husband and a Wife*; If he that has a Wife, shall unwittingly carry the Heart of a Female Crow, and if the woman well knowing it, shall carry about her the Heart of a Male Crow, *the Love between them will be inseparable*. And if you give to a Woman the Inwards of it roasted, she not knowing it, *she will love you well*. And if you anoint your Genital with its Brain and Honey, and shall lie with her, *she will love you entirely, and she will adhere to no man but your self*. Its Dung in wine, *cures difficulty in breathing*. Two spoonfuls of its blood drunk in wine, *perfectly cures the Dropsie*.

While others drew together strands of the magical tradition, the reformer Paracelsus was establishing a new one. He produced a flood of short works proposing reforms to religion, medicine, and alchemy – all of these interlinked. While most philosophers and physicians believed that material substances were made up of a combination of earth, water, air, and fire, Paracelsus claimed that the components were sulphur, salt, and mercury. Disease was caused by an impurity in one of these, and cures involved re-purification. As a result, many Paracelsian cures involved metals and minerals (traditional learned cures rarely did, typically consisting of herbal and animal products). For Paracelsus, disease existed because Adam and Eve had been banished from the Garden of Eden; at that point they had been told by an angel the secrets of medicine, but this information had been lost by the time of the ancient Greeks. As a result, real medical knowledge came not from reading ancient Greek books (as learned physicians did), but from direct experience of nature, and from talking to people who themselves had plenty of experience – such as wise women. The natural world was full of signs that God had left to show what substances were good to heal which parts of the body: a walnut could be expected to be good for the brain because it looked like a brain. This was the 'doctrine of signatures', and it underpinned a form of sympathetic magic that Paracelsians used in their medicine.

In fact, 'Paracelsianism' as a coherent system was compiled in the years after von Hohenheim's death, by his followers. They insinuated themselves into courts across Europe and reworked his texts to establish an overall doctrine that could be learned easily (and a canon of works that could be consulted). French Paracelsians even managed to have his remedies taught to students at the University of Montpellier – though a group working in Paris were blocked from similar action by the medical faculty there. Gradually, Paracelsian ideas caught hold across Europe, to the point where alchemical cures began to find their way into the most staunchly traditional of works. All the while, Paracelsians resurrected and translated into the vernacular magical works that they believed might prove useful, driving a renewal of interest in the subject.

Magi and cunning men

Learned writers referred to the practitioner of magic as a magus; others used terms such as 'cunning' or 'wise' men and women (*weise Männer* or *Frauen* in German), but the meaning, preserved in modern references to the 'wise men' who visited the biblical nativity, was essentially the same. Whatever one called them, they could carry out rites to help, to heal, and to uncover hidden information. They might be of high or low social status, rich or poor. Some worked for money, others would take no payment at all. They were present in communities across Europe; more than one commentator in early modern England suggested that there was perhaps one in every parish. Characteristic activities of cunning men and magi included, most pre-eminently, healing; astral magic to strengthen the body, ward against or fight disease, or acquire particular characteristics; cunning men in particular were also involved in such non-medical procedures as helping find lost objects and predicting the outcome of difficult enterprises or long journeys or voyages. Some magical practitioners tried to talk to angels, either for information of some kind or, in the case of some of the learned magi, to achieve mystical enlightenment. I will deal with these in turn.

Magic had long been a tool for the healer. The physician in Chaucer's *Canterbury Tales* used 'magyk natureel' and made 'ymages for his pacient', and such talismans (considered permissible by Aquinas, discussed by Ficino) were often used for medical ends. Some cures involved the practitioner or the sufferer reciting a formula, others had the sufferer wearing an amulet. Amulets were believed to protect against illnesses – sometimes any illness, sometimes a particular named problem. Magical remedies were used in a variety of circumstances, by learned healers just as happily as by others.

In the Renaissance, medicine remained an important reason for doing magic. Ficino's great magical work was the third part of a medical treatise *De vita* (*On Life*: the first two books were called *De vita sana*, *On a Healthy Life*, and *De vita longa*, *On a Long Life*). He concerned himself a great deal in the third book with restoring the spirit, which linked the soul to the body and received heavenly influences. Jupiter was particularly good for the spirit, he wrote, so it was important to eat Jovial foodstuffs: in these 'the sweetness is palpable and subtle', he explained, with 'a somewhat astringent and sharp taste' – almonds, hazelnuts, and pistachios, for instance, or licorice, raisins, partridge, or peacock meat. In the course of the work Ficino outlined a theory of the cosmos and its workings, but his primary intention was medical.

Pico was likewise interested in medicine, though his works give little clue to this. His library contained numerous medical tracts and at least one contemporary report describes him preparing a medicine for someone: Pietro Crinito wrote in his book of commonplaces *De honesta disciplina* (*On Virtuous Learning*, 1504) that when Pico's friend Ermolao Barbaro caught the plague, Pico sent him a remedy consisting of 'oil of scorpions and asps' tongues and other such poisons'.

The link between magus and medical practice was strong. Throughout the period, the main reason for going to see a 'cunning' man or woman was to be cured of an illness. Some cures involved prayer or prayer-like formulations. A 1604 letter records the remedy that Goodwife Veazy offered for 'ringworm, tetter-worm and canker-worm'. It consisted of saying, three times, 'In the name of God I begin and in the name of God I do end: thou tetter worm, or thou cankerworm begone from hence, in the name of the Father, of the Son and of the Holy Ghost', then applying honey and pepper. In 1617 Edmund Langdon, a medical practitioner around Bedminster, Somerset, gave a patient a piece of paper to wear as a protective charm, saying that it was so powerful that 'yf yt were hanged aboutt a cocks neck That then no man shold have the power to kill the said Cock'. These examples were repeated across Europe.

Magical procedures not involving written charms but supposed to act as cures included boiling eggs in urine, touching the sufferer (either simply by hand or with a staff), burning or burying a live animal, and other unlikely sounding procedures. The expertise of wise men and women was pre-eminent in cases where the cause itself might have been magical. Kiterell, a practitioner in mid-sixteenth-century Maidstone, was particularly known for dealing with bewitchment. Robert Booker, an unlicensed London healer examined by the College of Physicians in 1623, was recorded as having treated one patient he considered bewitched by anointing him with oil, giving him something to drink, and speaking a charm.

CAMPANELLA'S ADVICE ON ECLIPSES

Tommaso Campanella (1568–1639) aided the pope in preparing for an eclipse in 1628, to lessen its consequences. His guidelines were later published by political opponents to discredit him. The first recommendation was prayer and worship. The second was to close the house completely to prevent the 'bad air' (a dangerous outcome of the eclipse) from entering; inside, sprinkle 'with rose vinegar and the scents of spices', light a fire with bay, myrtle, rosemary, cypress and 'other aromatic woods'. Decorate with white silk cloths and branches. Light two lamps and five torches representing the planets (including the sun) – they would stay lit during the eclipse, making up for the loss of the eclipsed celestial body. Take companions whose birth charts are such that they will not themselves be affected by the eclipse. There should be music associated with Jupiter and Venus to help counteract the air's noxiousness, likewise 'stones, and plants, and colours, and scents, and music, and movements' that can help attract the influence of these beneficent planets. Use these to make distilled drinks that will possess useful astral powers. Do all this 'for three hours before the beginning of the eclipse, and for three after its end'.

Despite all this, medicine was far from the only activity of cunning men. Love magic, magic that caused an unsuspecting third party to love the wise man's client, had long been a staple of society at all levels. Prominent court cases occasionally revealed such practices among the elites. In 1441 Eleanor Cobham, the duchess of Gloucester, was accused of attempting to kill King Henry VI by necromancy. During the court proceedings it was revealed that in the past she had taken from Marjory Jourdemayne, the 'witch of Eye next Westminster', certain potions by which she had 'enforced' the duke 'to love her and to wedde her'. In the investigations following Sir Thomas Overbury's poisoning in the Tower in 1613, it was revealed that Frances, countess of Essex, and her friend Anne Turner, a physician's widow, had approached the astrological healer and alchemist Simon Forman (1552–1611) for love magic. The countess had sought the love of the earl of Somerset, Turner that of Sir Christopher Maynwaring. The same things were happening outside these circles; in 1582 Goodwife Swane of Margate was boasting of being able to concoct a drink 'which she saith if she give it to any young man that she liketh well of, he shall be in love with her', while a Lancashire yeoman called Alexander Atherton was claiming that he was the victim of a magical conspiracy to make him love Elizabeth Winstanley, and that his health was declining because she would not marry him.

Magic, and the divinatory procedures to which cunning men and magi were privy, provided ways of seeking things that had been lost. When the wife of John Redman of Sutton in Cambridgeshire left him in 1617, he was described as having gone 'from wizard to wizard, or, as they term them, "wise men", to have them bring her again'. Often what was to be found was buried treasure. The English courtier John Dee (1527–1608) believed that he could discover 'gold, silver, or better matter' by drawing on the 'sympathies and antipathies of things'; he was far from alone. In 1634, for instance, the Dean of Westminster Abbey allowed the king's clock-master, Davy Ramsey, to lead an expedition to search for treasure there, accompanied by the astrologer William Lilly and a diviner armed with a tool called 'Mosaical rods'.

Some of the things that could be found by these means had been intended to stay lost: solving cases of theft was another of the principal reasons for turning to a cunning man or woman. They employed the standard tools of divination, from the sieve and shears that non-specialists often used, balanced so that the sieve turned to select as the thief someone present or pick out a name read out from a list, to more sophisticated approaches such as looking in crystals or mirrors. A few practitioners summoned spirits to help. Under examination in 1566, John Walsh of Netherbury in Dorset admitted to having summoned a familiar spirit to locate stolen goods and reveal thieves' identities, providing the spirit with a live animal such as a chicken, cat, or dog in exchange for the information.

Ultimately, these 'wise' men and women provided whatever services were demanded of them. In mid-seventeenth-century Wiltshire, Thomas Mason received from a wise woman called Anne Bodenham (later prosecuted as a witch) a charm which, if worn, would apparently guard against bailiffs. In 1631 William Barckseale boasted to a group of six men who were hoping to steal from a ship at anchor in Southampton harbour that he could magically 'caste a deepe sleepe on the keepers of the shippe'. Magical aid, in the form of charms or otherwise, was bestowed to assist people financially, protect against violence, vermin, lightning, drunkenness, and prevent any other ill or bestow any good that might be identified.

The methods that these practitioners used tended to be broadly similar, from summoning spirits, reading the stars, and drawing down astral influences, to using virtues hidden in particular objects and substances. As Ficino explained so carefully (if not approvingly), the use of 'sigils' (drawn or engraved symbols) to harness the powers of the stars was an important way of achieving various results: guarding against or curing illnesses, strengthening or mitigating personal characteristics, by the selection of particular stars or constellations. These sigils went back far beyond Ficino; these were the items Aquinas had been considering when he ruled that those without writing might be natural, but those bearing words or letters must be communicating with an evil spirit. A particular image was imprinted on a sample of a suitable substance (particularly metal, possibly in a flat sheet – 'lamina' – or a ring). This was done at an astrologically significant moment to fix the desired astral influence in the item, which could then be worn. Symbols were combined for particular purposes, and the sigils were used to impart magical efficacy to other things: in 1597 Simon Forman prescribed one woman a potion into which a ring engraved with the symbol of Jupiter had been immersed. By such means, practitioners manipulated astral influences to their own ends.

Some sought communion with angels, either directly or (more usually) with the aid of a medium or 'scryer'. One well-known example was John Dee, a famed mathematician, astrologer, alchemist, and philosopher at the court of Elizabeth I, whose published works reveal an interest in the cabbala and a view of astral magic not unlike Ficino's. Dee owned a black obsidian mirror which now survives in the British Museum; this is shown in figure 2, along with a crystal ball which may resemble one used by Dee (but which cannot be authenticated as his), a gold disc engraved with a vision from an experiment in Cracow, and wax discs bearing magical images, symbols, and names, used as supports – the smaller discs for standing table legs on (there were originally four) and the larger for the 'shew-stone' itself. Dee only recorded having seen anything in them once, so he employed mediums to work with the items. Best known among these was 'Mr Talbot', actually Edward Kelley (1555–97?).

Figure 2 Some of the items with which John Dee practised magic

The 'spiritual conferences' (or 'actions') in which Kelley acted as an intermediary ran until 1587. They consisted of prayer and petitions, then waiting for Kelley to see something, and a prayer to close. Dee recorded details of these sessions (including the angels' reported speeches) assiduously. Sometimes others were present, including Albrecht Łaski, palatine of Sieradż, who visited England briefly and took Dee and Kelley with him when he left to return to Poland in 1583. The conferences were deeply influenced by existing magical literature: on one occasion in 1584 Dee reported having to reassure Kelley after his associate emerged 'speedily out of his study' carrying a copy of Agrippa's works which contained a passage suspiciously similar to what the angels had just told him. 'Whereupon he inferred that our spiritual instructors were coseners', Dee wrote, 'and therefore he would have no more to do with them.'

Dee and Kelley were (as Kelley reported) given angelic instructions to visit the Holy Roman Emperor Rudolf II in 1584, and once there, the angel Uriel (again via Kelley) told Dee to let the emperor know by letter that he could make the philosophers' stone. Dee also received from his assistant a number of texts in what he believed to be the world's original 'angelic' or 'Adamic' language. In 1587 Kelley announced (with some apparent reluctance) that they had been ordered to hold their wives in common. Dee was hesitant but eventually acquiesced; the men parted company shortly afterwards and Dee travelled back to England, and though he continued to hope for Kelley's return it was never to come.

Simon Forman also recorded having called up spirits and copied texts on how to learn from them. He referred to demons as 'spirits', calling them variously as part of a group or alone with the help of successive scryers. Through prayer or invocations he sought knowledge from these entities. Sometimes they refused to respond at all, while at one time he wrote that a spirit had appeared to him as a large black dog. Later Forman became interested in the *ars notoria* (see chapter 1), which provided him with supposedly angelic knowledge, and we know that from 1587 he started specifically calling angels. We have little information about his angelic conversations, though he wrote of speaking to one called 'Raziel', who had presented Adam with a book of astronomy and magic later discovered by Solomon.

There are other examples of engagement with spirits that participants determined to be angelic. A pamphlet published in 1659 reported a wonderful cure achieved by someone following the advice of an unknown old man subsequently identified as an angel. Many cunning folk and a number of sectaries around that same turbulent time claimed angelic informants. Manuscript texts in circulation explained the rituals and the tools (such as swords, wands, candles) to be employed in summoning such spirits for consultation.

Some believed that the best route would be to use the philosophers' stone, the ultimate achievement of alchemy, which (in one form, at least) was sometimes understood to allow the subject to see angels. Robert Boyle, the famous experimentalist and founding member of the Royal Society of London, certainly accepted this, and the belief was also recorded by Elias Ashmole (1617–92) in his *Theatrum chemicum Britannicum* of 1652. It was not always this way round; William Lilly, for one, held that producing the stone in the first place was impossible without possessing secrets vouchsafed by angels.

Seeking angels was not always about power over (or knowledge of) the natural world. Plato had suggested that magic was knowledge of the gods, and some early modern scholars concurred: 'the art of *Magicke*', Sir Walter Raleigh wrote, 'is the art of worshipping God.' Pico claimed that natural magic excited in its practitioner 'an admiration for the works of God', from which 'charity, faith and hope' certainly followed. For nothing, he added, advanced 'the worship of God more than the incessant contemplation of God's wonders'. Worshipping and contemplating God lay at the heart of Pico's conception of magic, and Dee's likewise. For all that this magic was a practical activity centred on nature, religion and contemplation were still of central importance.

Reputation, legend, and literature

It was the practical activities that outsiders tended to focus on, however, in their approbation of supposed magicians. Trithemius, Agrippa, Paracelsus, Dee; only four of the best-known examples, these men attracted considerable rumour and legend attacking their characters and attributing to them shocking deeds.

Trithemius was already known for his scholarship and piety when he acquired his reputation for magical practice. Much of that reputation, ironically, was connected with a book he had written on cryptography and the sending of disguised messages;

it employed sufficiently mysterious symbols that many readers identified it as demonic, and it was eventually placed on the Catholic Church's index of prohibited books. Written around 1499, it was not printed until 1606. Around the time of its completion, Trithemius wrote to Arnold Bostius, a Carmelite monk in Ghent, Flanders, but Bostius died before receiving the letter and the prior of the monastery opened it and allowed it to be copied. In the letter, Trithemius had written that he could communicate messages secretly without the messenger's knowledge, or without a messenger. Rumours concerning his claimed abilities, embellished, spread rapidly throughout France and Germany: Trithemius was left publicly denying that he could raise the dead, tell the future, or perform a number of other dubious actions, while other scholars concluded that to achieve any of these he must have demonic aid. Charles de Bovelles, the best student of another magical writer (Jacques Lefèvre d'Étaples 1450–1536), visited Trithemius in Sponheim in 1503 and studied the book in question, only to decide that it was about conjuring demons and that Trithemius was engaged in demonic magic – though it seems from the friendly letter that Trithemius wrote to him two years later that he remained unaware of this conclusion.

The reputation that attached to Heinrich Cornelius Agrippa was darker still. The first problem was his publication history: he described and defended occult learning in his *Three Books of Occult Philosophy* (completed 1510), then attacked it in the late 1520s in a work *On the Uncertainty and Vanity of the Arts and Sciences*. He then had the works printed in reverse order. As a result, neither contemporaries nor modern scholars have ever been very certain what his views really were, and whether they changed or how. John French, who translated the *Three Books* into English in the middle of the seventeenth century, pointed out that the attack on magic was part of a piece of rhetoric intended to emphasise that the only certainty was in God's word. James Sanford, however, who translated the later work into English, remarked that though Agrippa's knowledge had been great, he had given his mind to 'unleeful [unlawful] Artes, contrarie to the Lawes of God and man', and many readers agreed. According to one, Gabriel Harvey, 'Agrippa was reputed a gyant in confutation, a demi-god in omni-sufficiency of knowledge, [and] a diuell in the practise of horrible Artes'. Agrippa's cause was not helped by the Italian historian Paolo Giovio, who in 1546 reported rumours to the effect that he had used magic to help the emperor's armies to victory; that when someone had died in his house he commanded a demon to inhabit the body and walk it outside so that the man would appear to have collapsed there instead; and that at his death he had been abandoned even by the 'evil genius' (spirit) that had attended him in canine form. As the seventeenth-century writer Samuel Butler put it:

> Agrippa kept a Stygian-Pug,
> I'th' garb and habit of a *Dog*,
> That was his *Tutor*; and the *Curr*
> Read to th'occult *Philosopher*,
> And taught him subtly to maintain
> All other Sciences are vain.

This was the way a great many in early modern Europe saw Agrippa: a necromancer, in league with demons and accompanied by a familiar in the shape of a black dog.

While Agrippa was arguably a victim of rumour and misunderstanding, Paracelsus to a large extent was author of his own misfortune. In his lifetime he was known for his pugnacity as well as his iconoclasm and he was widely reviled. Unsurprisingly his claims that university physic was worthless were rejected by university physicians. He lasted only months as a lecturer at Basel. For his later followers the situation was little different: in the scholastic world, the term 'Paracelsista' was an insult, a pejorative word used to denigrate those who wanted to overturn the treasured intellectual systems of the universities.

John Dee attracted trouble both official and public. His May 1555 arrest on the order of the privy council was initially for calculating the birth-charts of the king, queen, and Princess Elizabeth; later this charge became conjuring and witchcraft, and when one of the accusers lost a child and found another stricken with blindness, rumours of a familiar spirit grew. Dee was released into the custody of the bishop of London in August and convinced him of his orthodoxy. While travelling on the continent in 1586 he was banished from the dominions of the Holy Roman Emperor after the intervention of the papal nuncio. In his absence his library at Mortlake was raided, probably by former associates, and he lost many books and instruments. He spent his later years in increasing poverty and, apparently, disfavour. Like Agrippa, however, Dee suffered a worse reputation after death than during life. An ill-wisher hoping to expose him as having conversed not with angels but demons edited and printed his 'spiritual conferences' in 1659; but although the project met with some measure of success there are also indications that it encouraged much imitation.

A striking view of the Renaissance magus was produced by Christopher Marlowe, who dramatised the legend of Johann Faust early in the seventeenth century as *The Tragical History of Doctor Faustus*. In Marlowe's account Faustus, a learned man at the University of Wittenberg, has risen to the heights that the arts and medicine will allow, and is disillusioned with law and divinity (remarking of the former: 'This study fits a mercenary drudge'). Necromancy, however, is 'heavenly' to him, opening 'a world of profit and delight / Of power, of honour, of omnipotence'. 'A sound magician is a demi-god', he adds. Encouraged by the characters 'Valdes' and 'Cornelius' (presumably named after Agrippa), he determines to 'practise magic and concealed arts'; Cornelius explains that an astrologer with knowledge of languages and minerals 'Hath all the principles magic doth require'. Faustus conjures up Mephistophilis and signs a pact that promises his soul in exchange for years of service; the play ends as payment is taken – Faustus damned despite reassurances from friends that he could repent and recant and still escape his fate.

In stark contrast is the character of Prospero in Shakespeare's *The Tempest*, written at around the same time. Prospero's helpers are spirits rather than demons; Ariel is a spirit but there is nowhere any suggestion that he is evil. He has been imprisoned by the former occupant of Prospero's island, the witch Sycorax, and freed by Prospero using his magic to undo hers. Prospero's account to his daughter Miranda of his exile charts a progression not dissimilar to that of Faustus. While initially he was 'so reported / In dignity, and for the liberal arts/Without a parallel', he went on to set aside the government of his state, 'being transported / And rapt in secret studies'. His power derives from the written word; as Caliban advises his co-conspirators:

> Remember
> First to possess his books, for without them
> He's but a sot as I am, nor hath not
> One spirit to command – they all do hate him
> As rootedly as I.

Yet Ariel is faithful to Prospero, and is eventually freed for his dutiful service. The famous speech in which Prospero announces his intention to abandon his art places emphasis again on books and equipment:

> this rough magic
> I here abjure. And when I have required
> Some heavenly music – which even now I do –
> To work mine end upon their senses that
> This airy charm is for, I'll break my staff,

> Bury it certain fathoms in the earth,
> And deeper than did ever plummet sound
> I'll drown my book.

Real-life magi lived out such patterns themselves. Jacques Lefèvre d'Étaples, having written a book on natural magic, eventually decided that: 'It is nonsense to believe that any magic is natural or good, for natural magic is a wicked deception practised by men who seek to hide their crimes under a respectable name.' The importance of such abjurations to the myth of the magus, however, makes it hard to tell how far such about-turns have been read into the sources by overenthusiastic historians. Pico wrote a work attacking astrology late in life, but it is open to question whether this was a product of the same magical worldview he had espoused all along, or an attack on that view. We have already examined the curious relationship between Agrippa's extensive study *Three Books of Occult Philosophy* and his later diatribe against all learning. For the purposes of plotting out Agrippa's intellectual biography, much rests on the question of whether the subsequent enlargement and printing of the *Three Books* reflected a change of heart or a change of financial circumstances. Whatever the truth of these cases, they reveal the strength of the myths surrounding magi – for us as much as for contemporaries.

The Hermetic corpus

Practitioners of magic had their own view of the archetypal magus, and it resembled the ancient sage Hermes Trismegistus. Brief mystical and alchemical tracts had circulated under his name during the Middle Ages. Best known was the 'Emerald Tablet', a list of cryptic aphorisms: 'what is below is as what is above, and what is above is as what is below, for performing miracles of one thing', it went, and the expression 'as above, so below' recurs throughout magical writings from the medieval period on. Readers believed Hermes himself to have been an Egyptian sage contemporary with Moses, and the original source of Plato's ideas about the world. He had apparently anticipated the coming of Christ, and set doctrines resembling Christian teachings in the context of a magical cosmos. So when in 1463 Marsilio Ficino's patron Cosimo de' Medici handed him a full collection of Hermes' works, rediscovered in a Byzantine copy, he ordered Ficino to set aside his project translating Plato into Latin and instead concentrate on the older and more important 'Hermetic corpus'. The result was a Latin version, published in 1471. The collection unveiled divine wisdom disclosed in prophetic dreams, hidden knowledge of the mysterious links and influences of the cosmos. It was an account that provided a model for learned magi across Renaissance Europe.

How much influence the Hermetic texts actually exercised is a contentious issue. The idea of a 'Hermetic tradition' of practitioners who believed in and followed them was put forward by the historian Frances Yates. She argued that these works were the foundation for a magical tradition that stretched from Ficino's astral magic, to Pico (who took a similar approach but added the cabbala), to Agrippa. Since Yates's work it has become increasingly clear that the Hermetic texts were more an inspiration than a guide. Ficino's own writings on magic actually demonstrate little debt to the corpus. The name Hermes itself is mentioned, briefly, in only two of the twenty-six chapters of his work; instead Ficino derives his account largely (and explicitly) from the Neoplatonists he had spent so long reading, and whose translations he would publish in the following decade. Secondly, Pico's magic was not Ficino's plus the cabbala – partly because it differed in important ways from Ficino's magic, but mainly because Pico produced his work first. Pico actually mentioned the Hermetic corpus no more than Ficino had. Successive generations of writers on magic drew inspiration from the

Hermetic texts, but Hermes was only one of several precursors to whom they could appeal. His principal role was to be admired and imitated.

Then, in 1614, his reputation was severely dented. The culprit was Isaac Casaubon (1559–1614), a renowned scholar working on a Protestant response to Cardinal Cesare Baronio's vast recent Catholic history of the Church. Only one volume was ever printed (responding to the first half of the first volume of Baronio's twelve-volume work) before Casaubon died, but that book included a detailed attack on the traditional dating of the Hermetic corpus. Baronio had included Hermes among a number of non-biblical prophets who had foretold the coming of Christ; in response, Casaubon explained at length that the Hermetic texts could not be as old as usually believed, and argued that they did not predate Christ at all (so that, no matter how explicitly they referred to Christ, they could not be prophecies). He pointed out that neither Plato nor Aristotle, nor any other authors of pagan antiquity, had mentioned Hermes Trismegistus, and wrote that though there might well have been someone by that name he could not have been the author of the works now ascribed to him. The Hermetic corpus looked like Plato's philosophy because it had been *influenced by* Plato and the Neoplatonists, not because it had predated them, and the same went for the parts that resembled biblical passages. There were echoes of books from both the Old and New Testaments, Psalms and liturgies, and even works of the early Church Fathers. The Hermetic texts, Casaubon concluded, had been written by Christian (or somewhat Christian) authors in Christianity's early years, to make their teachings acceptable to those they were trying to convert. As further proof, Casaubon noted references to and quotations from Greeks who clearly postdated Hermes, and went in detail over the late-Greek style and vocabulary. The Hermetic writings had not been written by an ancient Egyptian and were not prophecies of Christ.

As clear as this demolition was, its position in the middle of a detailed critique of a twelve-volume Latin Church history was hardly a public platform. Casaubon's argument had precious little immediate effect. An English translation of the texts was published thirty-five years later. Athanasius Kircher (1601–80), a prodigious and respected Jesuit scholar, remained convinced that Hermes had been an ancient Egyptian sage. Even readers who were well aware of Casaubon's argument were not always wholly convinced; Isaac Newton remained sure that the texts at least contained antique doctrine, even if they were in a more modern form. Nonetheless, by the beginning of the eighteenth century the standing of the Hermetic corpus was waning, and its opponents now had serious ammunition with which to attack it. Ignoring Casaubon's attack became an increasingly untenable position.

Whatever their influence, the Hermetic texts plotted a parallel course to learned natural magic. They had emerged at around the same time; now they declined at around the same time. We still have no wholly adequate explanation for magic's fall from grace, but it simply became intellectually unrespectable. Cunning folk still practised it throughout the Western world, but by the eighteenth century few scholars took it seriously. By the mid-1700s neither the Hermetic texts nor learned magic commanded a great deal of respect.

The Yates thesis

One possible explanation for magic's fate among European scholars is that it did not disappear – it became science. According to Frances Yates, magic was not simply a flawed precursor of science, but actually its source. The 'Yates thesis' runs roughly as follows. The scholarly study of nature through the Middle Ages and Renaissance was known as natural philos-

ophy, and it was precisely that: a type of philosophy. Its proponents read Aristotle, considered the normal course of nature and
its workings, and debated with one another, employing carefully
constructed, scrupulously logical arguments. By and large, they
did not carry out practical tests. Natural magic, in contrast, was
about intervention in the material world. It often involved what
had long been called 'experiments': procedures whose results
were known through experience rather than predicted from
books or by logic. It was important in magic to know how to
bring about particular events; it was not important to know why
or how a procedure worked. The magus was interested primarily in knowing that a given cause produced a particular effect; he
would try things out and generalize from specific instances. The
Hermetic texts advocated this sort of active approach to nature,
utterly unlike the contemplative practices of philosophers in the
universities. In the seventeenth century, however, scholars
turned to a new kind of natural philosophy: this was centred on
experiments, by which (in the words of Francis Bacon) they
could 'put nature to the rack': physically interrogate it to acquire
knowledge. Experimental philosophers would, like Renaissance
magi, test the natural world to add to their knowledge. As Yates
herself put it, the Renaissance magical tradition, and in particular the fascination with Hermes Trismegistus, stimulated 'the
will towards genuine science and its operations'.

In the years since Yates produced her theory, a lot more
work has been done on the relationship between magic and
natural philosophy, as well as on the changes that natural philosophy underwent during the sixteenth and seventeenth centuries.
We are in a much better position now to examine the overlap
between magic and the new experimental natural philosophy.
Of critical importance were the properties of matter. According
to most philosophers in the medieval universities, magic was by
its very nature excluded from philosophy. Thinking, they
claimed, involved calling up mental images, which meant that it

was impossible to think about things that couldn't be seen, heard, felt, smelt, or tasted. Accordingly, the qualities inherent in matter were divided into two classes: 'manifest' qualities, which could be sensed and therefore thought about – colour, for instance, or smell; and hidden (in Latin, 'occultus') qualities, such as magnetism, which were insensible and therefore unthinkable. This placed them squarely outside the realm of philosophical investigation, outside of natural philosophy. Scholars studying nature, according to these principles, had no option but to concentrate on understanding manifest properties. Those who speculated on occult qualities and their causes were in a difficult position: they might claim divine inspiration (perhaps via Hermes), or they might be accused of learning from demons.

This distinction between occult and manifest qualities came under increasing fire during the seventeenth century, as long-held attitudes to nature were overturned and new philosophies gained ground. The French philosopher René Descartes rejected the suggestion that the cause of colour was any more 'manifest' than the cause of magnetism – but he was happy to propose an explanation for both. According to Descartes, colours and magnetism were both caused by the movement of tiny particles too small to see. Supporters of this view of nature, the so-called 'mechanical philosophy', hailed its ability to explain occult qualities when the traditional philosophy of the universities had sidelined them. Mechanical philosophers were able to investigate and propose explanations of occult qualities that had previously been the preserve of writers on magic.

A number of English philosophers were content to leave some qualities unexplained, provided that they could be confirmed experimentally. The most famous example was Isaac Newton, who (much to the irritation of his continental rival Gottfried Wilhelm Leibniz) introduced the idea that inherent in matter was a mysterious attractive force he called 'gravity'.

Newton's calculations showed that it must be there, but he provided no explanation of how it functioned – mechanical or otherwise. To Newton, admitting that matter had one or two mysterious properties was an improvement on adding an extra one for every new phenomenon encountered; for Leibniz, Newton's refusal to propose an account of how gravity worked made it no better than an occult quality. Newton responded that what had been objectionable about occult qualities was not that philosophers had offered no causal explanation for them, but that they had claimed that the causes were unknowable. In these debates, in the redrawing of the relationship between the visible and the intelligible, in the embracing of previously magical phenomena by philosophers, and in the shift in attitudes towards explanation and experiment, we can see hints of Yates's link between magic and modern science. That is hardly a complete endorsement, of course. Did magic provide the impetus for experiment? There is little evidence to suggest that it did, and there are other plausible candidates. Science took over from learned natural magic, but it seems unlikely that magic *generated* science or the approach to nature that it embodies.

While exercising power over nature was an important part of Renaissance magic, so was display: creating spectacle and illusion, through machinery, sleight of hand, and deception. Magic had always involved trickery – even charlatanry. The magician was often a trickster, sometimes an entertainer. The next chapter looks at this tradition and the rise of stage magic.

3
Tricks and illusions

According to Heinrich Cornelius Agrippa, the art of illusions was part of magic: the 'Juglers skil' he called it, using a term that until recently denoted stage magic rather than feats of throwing and catching. By illusions, he went on, 'Magitiens doo shewe vaine visions', and 'plaie many miracles'; they did this not through incantations and devilish rituals, but by 'a readie subteltie and nimblenesse of the handes'. Writing more than a century and a half later, John Aubrey concurred; he began a chapter on 'Magick' in his collection of customs and folklore with a discussion of deception by sleight of hand and mechanical contrivances, under the heading 'Tergetors (or Tregetors)' – another old word for illusionists, used as far back as Chaucer. Illusion by hidden contraptions or trickery was part of magic because magic was often defined as the production of impressive effects from hidden causes. In Pico's words, magic helped nature work wonders by 'calling up' the world's hidden powers 'from their hiding places into the light'. Using hidden powers to work wonders was a description that could apply equally well to what we call 'tricks' as much as to the 'experiments' of the last chapter. It was particularly during the eighteenth and nineteenth centuries, however, that the illusionist emerged as a theatrical entertainer, with an identity distinct from and even opposed to the practitioners of 'real' magic. The word 'conjuror' is a useful one: in the seventeenth century it was used universally to mean someone who summoned demons; by the end of the eighteenth it had come to refer to a performer who entertained through illusions.

Much of the history of magic has been concerned with spectacle – with magic as show. This chapter traces the history of magical performances from the wondrous devices and courtly magic of the Middle Ages to the televised acts of the modern magician.

Magic and mechanics

As natural magic (at least according Agrippa's definition) was the harnessing of nature's forces and processes to produce wonderful effects, the use of hidden mechanisms and intricate mechanical devices could be considered magical. Agrippa called the use of these machines 'mathematical magic'. His examples included a flying wooden dove constructed by an ancient Greek philosopher and mathematician called Archytas (428–347 BC), and a 'Brasen [i.e. brass] heade forged by *Albert* the great, which as it is saide did speake'. Many Renaissance commentators wrote of these deeds; some claimed to have equalled them. Robert Fludd (1574–1637) announced that he had personally built a bellowing wooden bull, as well as a moving dragon and a lyre that played itself. It is difficult to assess the truth of such statements but what indications there are suggest a large degree of exaggeration.

Whatever the truth of experts' capabilities, the rumours bred fear. John Dee (1527–1609) dated the evil reputation that dogged him throughout his life back to the construction at university in 1547 of a flying scarab for a performance of Aristophanes' play *Peace*. The scarab flew 'up to Jupiter's pallace, with a man and his basket of victualls on her back', Dee explained, 'whereat was great wondring, and many vaine reportes spread abroad of the meanes how that was effected'. Even after all this time, the accusations of devilry rankled: should anyone who achieved such feats 'Naturally, Mathematically, and Mechanically', he asked, 'be counted and called a "Conjurer"?' Such accusations extended to people who certainly did not think

AGRIPPA ON MATHEMATICAL MAGIC

Agrippa, in a contemporary English translation of *De incertitudine*, devoted a brief chapter to 'Mathematical Magicke'. He wrote of some:

> very prudente and aduenturous searchers of nature, whiche, without natural vertues, with ye *Mathematical* disciplines alone, the influences of the heauens beinge put thereto, do promisse that they are able to bringe forthe thinges like to the woorkes of nature, as bodies that go [and] speake, whiche for al that haue not the vertues of the soule ... I suppose that is spoken of these skilles, which *Plato* saithe in the xj. Booke of his Lawes: menne haue an Arte, whereby they brought foorthe certaine latter thinges, not partakinge of the veritie, [and] diuinitie, but made certaine semblaunces muche like to themselues: and the *Magitians* very presumptuous parsons haue gone so farre to do all thinges, especially with the fauoure of that auncient and terrible Serpent the promiser of scie[n]ces, that like to him, as Apes they endeuoure to counterfaite God and nature.

of themselves as involved in magic, natural or otherwise. John Rowley reported in 1651 having been accused of 'Sorcery and Conjuration' by a priest who spotted him measuring the height of a church steeple with a surveying instrument. Religious reformers in England in 1538 claimed to have discovered that a crucifix at the Abbey of Boxley in Kent, famous for miraculously moving, was actually a mechanical device operated by hidden monks. Whatever denials the abbey's inhabitants might proffer, such accusations played into the Protestant suspicion that Catholics were heavily involved in the practice of magic; at least one contemporary, who witnessed the discovery, referred to the operator as a 'juggler'. John Aubrey remarked that 'the vulgar' truly believed that the Elizabethan mathematician Thomas Allen was 'a Conjurer' because he kept 'a great many Mathematicall Instruments and Glasses in his Chamber'. According to Aubrey, Allen's watch, left on a windowsill, had spooked the maids with its ticking; they had 'concluded that that was his Devill' and thrown it out of the window into the moat. Aubrey further claimed that this was not an unusual connection to make: authorities 'burned Mathematical bookes for Conjuring bookes'. 'In those darke times', he explained, 'Astrologer, Mathematician, and Conjurer were accounted the same things.'

All of these complaints assumed that mechanical devices, however ingenious and complex, were not magical. Robert Recorde, for instance, believed that Roger Bacon 'was accompted so greate a negromancier' simply because he 'was in geometrie and other mathematicall sciences so experte, that he coulde dooe by theim such thynges as were wonderfull in the syght of most people'. John Wilkins (1614–72) called his 1648 book of machinery and devices *Mathematicall Magick*, explaining that this was because 'the art of such Mechanicall inventions ... hath been formerly so styled, and in allusion to vulgar opinion, which doth commonly attribute all such strange operations unto the power of Magic'. His contemporary Walter Charleton (1620–1707) described how Wilkins and several associates

> practise all Delusions of the sight, in the Figures, Magnitudes, Motions, Colours, Distances, and Multiplications of Objects: And, were you there, you might be entertained with such admirable Curiosities ... as former ages would have been startled at, and believed to have been Magical ... And, were *Friar* [Roger] *Bacon* alive again, he would with amazement confesse, that he was canonized a Conjurer, for effecting far lesse, than these men frequently exhibit to their friends, in sport.

Such truly knowledgeable and skilled people as these could copy or best magical feats, but they were not actually performing magic. This was a long way from Agrippa's notion of natural magic, which included hidden mechanisms that produced wonderful effects; for Wilkins and Charleton, machinery appeared magic only to the 'vulgar'. Mechanics, as the eighteenth century approached, had become a way of imitating magic, or a means of achieving feats that might be mistaken for magic by those too deluded or ill-educated to know otherwise. Magic was not wonder-producing: magic was what wonder-producing arts were *mistaken for* by the uninitiated.

Courtly magic

Generating wonders to produce spectacle was a central concern of many courtiers, and courts both real and imaginary hosted magical performers. Chrétien de Troyes (*c*.1140–*c*.1190) listed them among the minstrels entertaining at the fictional wedding of Erec and Enide, surrounded by singers, musicians, and acrobats; in the original Old French the magical performers 'anchante', enchant. Christopher Marlowe had Faustus conjure the likeness of Alexander the Great for the German emperor. Heinrich Cornelius Agrippa spent much of his life at various European courts. In *The Unfortunate Traveller* (1594), Thomas Nashe had his hero Jacke Wilton visit the University of Wittenberg and find 'that abundant scholler *Cornelius Agrippa*', who was famed as 'the greatest coniurer in Christendome'. '*Scoto*' (presumably Girolamo Scotto, 1505–72), 'that did the iugling trickes before the Queene', Nashe added, 'never came neere him one quarter in magicke reputation.' In this story, which Nashe drew from previous authors, Agrippa went on to call up Cicero to deliver an oration. Scotto himself, a musician who seems to have engaged in some kind of legerdemain, was scarcely luckier in his posthumous reputation. James I claimed in his *Daemonologie* (1597) that the performer had acted with the devil's help.

For obvious economic reasons, grandees were often the patrons and recipients of automata and spectacular machinery. The mechanical fly and eagle created in Nuremberg by Regiomontanus were both presented to the Holy Roman Emperor Maximilian I. A banquet held in 1549 at the famed fêtes at Binche in the Low Countries by the Queen Dowager, Mary of Austria, in celebration of the formal recognition of Prince Philip of Spain as heir to the Holy Roman Empire, took place in an 'Enchanted Chamber' where a layered table bearing food descended from the ceiling, while overhead mechanical stars and planets moved and a rain of perfume fell. Courts across Europe were adorned with clocks, table fountains, and other ornaments that had been turned into or decorated with moving figures.

Renaissance courts in particular saw even more grandiose constructions than these. In 1598 Henri IV of France sought a mechanical water-garden for a series of terraces leading down from behind the palace at Saint-Germain-en-Laye to the river Seine. They were designed for him by the architect Tommaso Francini, lent to Henri for the purpose by the Florentine Archduke Ferdinand I de Medici, and comprised a fountain, channels and reservoirs, and several grottoes containing moving figures such as Perseus descending from the ceiling to slay a dragon, or Bacchus drinking on a barrel. The mechanisms were driven by the force of the water's flow. Michel de Montaigne, in his account of travelling through Italy, described similar scenes (though on a much smaller scale) at two major villas there. Much grander were the pageants that welcomed the king of Spain and Holy Roman Emperor Charles V to London in the summer of 1522; according to a contemporary, one included a model island populated with plants and animals. 'And att the comyng off the emprowr the bestys dyd move and goo, the fisshes dyd sprynge, the byrdes dyd synge'.

We should not limit ourselves to 'jugglers' and mechanics, and the clearly performative side of magic. Many of the experiments that survive in necromancy handbooks are intended to produce illusions, and in particular to give rise to unreal visions. The so-called 'Munich handbook' of necromancy lists two procedures which were clearly intended for use at court. One was making a banquet appear (though not actually come into being, the food providing no nourishment regardless of how much might be consumed). The other, accompanied by a somewhat unlikely account of its use before the emperor, was causing demons disguised as armed men to attack then creating (the appearance of) a castle to protect against them. These were potentially spectacular but morally reprehensible. In similar fashion, the presumption in cases such as the legend that Cicero had enacted an oration at Agrippa's behest was that demons were either taking Cicero's place, or somehow deceiving the senses of onlookers to make them believe that they were seeing what they were not.

One of the fascinating aspects of courtly magic is the closeness of the relationship – lack of distinction, even – between the court magician as performer or expert in mechanical deception, and the court magician as magus, expert in manipulating hidden powers or calling on spirits. Chaucer, in his 'Franklin's Tale', had a character suggest that his brother Aurelius seek the aid of an expert in magic and illusion. The woman whom Aurelius sought to marry had declared that he must first clear the rocks from the coast of Brittany; but this might be possible, his brother explained, by the same skills with which 'thise subtile tregetoures playe': these entertainers had often (he had heard) made water and a barge appear in large halls, or spring meadow flowers, or stone castles; and made these things disappear afterwards too. In fact, we have records of such displays: in 1378

Charles V of France organised for his uncle, the Holy Roman Emperor Charles IV, the re-enactment of the capture of Jerusalem by Godfrey of Boulogne, complete with arrival in a large ship. The word Chaucer uses, 'tregetour', captures in its range of meanings the ambivalence of such figures in courtly life. The Middle English word referred to magic in the sense of sorcery, and to magic in the sense of 'juggling', trickery – to deceive or for entertainment. These were courtiers whose typical role was to entertain, but who might prove dangerous foes or valuable allies.

Jugglers

Not all magical performers were courtiers. Some set themselves up at fairs and markets practising sleight of hand and illusions for profit. This 'juggling' took place across early modern Europe and involved basic types of fraud. The 'ball and cup' game seems to have been played from at least the late fifteenth century; several portrayals survive in German pictures, concerned chiefly with scorning those who were duped into taking part. The juggler shared skills with cheats and criminals: one late sixteenth-century author noted that the pickpocket 'exceeds the jugler for agilitie, and hath his *legiar de maine* as perfectly'. Churchmen warned of their baleful and dangerous influence. St Bernard of Clairvaux (1090–1153), the French founder of the Cistercian Order, told a correspondent: 'I have heard that jugglers visit you – beware what happens. A man turning to jugglers will soon have a wife whose name is poverty.' When they speak, he added, 'pretend not to hear and think of other things'. Juggling was also linked to devilry, often self-consciously by its practitioners. In the mid-seventeenth century a writer called Thomas Ady explained that because 'the common tradition and foolish opinion' held that a familiar spirit in physical form must be attendant for 'the doing of strange things', a juggler would carry something that would look like an 'imp' – such as 'the skin of a mouse stopped with feathers' and with a spring in its base. He would then bounce this around while talking to it: 'I will make you stay, would you be gone?' This 'spirit' would then help him in his feats.

The kinds of exercise under discussion dated back to at least the late Middle Ages. A monk at Syon Abbey in Middlesex late in the fifteenth century, Thomas Betson, wrote into his notebook a number of what we would now call 'tricks' – ways in which, he explained, you could deceive people into thinking you were performing magic. A fine hair from a woman's head, for instance, could be used to move a coin or suspend an egg invisibly. This and other sources explain how to make inanimate objects move (in Betson's case, make an apple rock by placing a beetle in a hole at its core), how to cause various impressive optical illusions and effects with light, how to make someone itch, and so on. Codified in texts from around the fourteenth century onwards, the status of such procedures was questionable. Though Betson was clear that they did not count as magic, others disagreed, and instructions were often included within manuscripts containing lore of a more unequivocally magical nature.

Jugglers were visually distinctive. Henry Chettle, in *Kindharts Dreame* (London, 1592), described a juggler as wearing a 'round lowe crownd rent silke hat' with a band 'knit in many knotes, wherein stucke two round stickes after the Iuglers manner'. He had a leather jerkin, yellow and blue hose, and a cloak of three colours. They often also carried a bag around their waists, to carry items and sometimes to help things disappear.

We know something of the performances of jugglers from contemporary accounts. An Italian observer noted in 1550 that they were able to move and hide things, to eat glass, to stick things into their arms and hands, to pull nails out of their mouths, to link chains without breaking them and to eat or blow fire. In one trick, a boy's head appeared to be separated from his body without killing him.

One well-known juggler in early seventeenth-century England was William Vincent. The earliest reference to him is in 1619, when he was granted a licence 'to exercise the art of Legerdemaine in any Townes within the Relme of England & Ireland'; the last record of his activity is from 1642 when he performed in Coventry. He seems to have been well known for his performances, which (according to contemporary references) involved such feats as swallowing and regurgitating daggers as well as straightforward legerdemain, making things disappear and appear, and seem also to have included more acrobatic displays. His stage name, a term that spread rapidly to become shorthand, first for a magician and later for the practice of magic itself, was 'Hocus Pocus'. Contemporaries might remark of a budding juggler or slippery deceiver that 'he is a very *Hocus Pocus* indeed'. He gained fame throughout the kingdom through his name, his feats – and his characteristic stage patter. According to *Hocvs Pocvs Ivnior*, a contemporary book that he may have written, a juggler 'must have strange termes, and emphaticall words, to grace, and adorne his actions, and the more to astonish the beholders'. A 1650 epitaph played a little on the way he talked on stage:

Here *Hocas* lies with his tricks and his knocks.
Whom death hath made sure as his Juglers box:
Who many hath cozen'd by his leiger-demain,
Is presto convey'd and here underlain:
Thus *Hocas* he's here, and here he is not,
While death plaid the *Hocas*, and brought him toth pot.

Even in its most renowned exponents, juggling was scarcely separable from cheating and deception on the one hand, and devilry and magic on the other. Vincent was known as a cardsharp

THE DECOLLATION OF JOHN THE BAPTIST

One spectacular trick performed by early modern jugglers was, as Reginald Scot put it, 'To cut off ones head, and to laie it in a platter'; performers referred to it as the 'decollation' of John the Baptist.

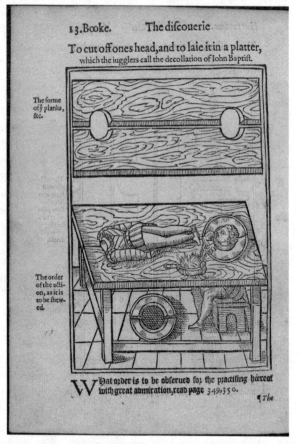

Figure 3 The equipment for the 'Decollation of John the Baptist'

> ## THE DECOLLATION OF JOHN THE BAPTIST (cont.)
>
> The image in figure 3 is from *The Discouerie of Witchcraft*. An arrangement of boarding resembling a set of stocks, with two neck-holes, was to be set on its side as a table-top and dressed with a tablecloth bearing matching holes; a 'platter' with its centre removed was placed over the top of that. Then, 'having these in readinesse', explained *Hocvs Pocvs Ivnior*, 'you must have two boyes; the one must lie along the table with his back upward, and he must put his head thorow the one hole of the table, cloth and all; the other must sit under the table and put his head thorow the other hole of the table ...' It was possible 'to make the sight more dreadfull to behold' by creating veins from strands of material, smearing the area with sheep's blood and placing small pieces of liver on the platter.

and was accused of fraud following a game in 1630. Reginald Scot (1538?–99), writing on witchcraft, noted that a contemporary juggler called Bornelio Feats was also a 'witch or conjurer, euerie waie a cousener: his qualities and feats were to me and manie other well knowne and detected'. These were associations that their successors would have to work hard to abandon.

In broad terms, however, Scot did not count 'juggling' as 'magic'. He dissociated them carefully (though what we might call 'tricks' and 'experiments' were transmitted side by side in manuscripts), and suggested that performers should end by informing audiences that their deeds were 'no supernaturall actions, but deuises of men'. He explained the basis of much of what jugglers did as 'consisting in fine and nimble conueiance, called legerdemaine: as when they seeme to cast awaie, or to deliuer to another that which they reteine still in their owne hands'. He also noted the importance of confederacy, defining 'priuate' confederacy as when a deed supposedly performed miraculously in front of the crowd had actually been achieved secretly beforehand, and 'publike' confederacy when the juggler had made a secret pact with audience members (or, occasionally, had trained animals) to assist him. Scot's *Discouerie of Witchcraft* (1584) was written to show that what were often accorded demonic explanations were actually achieved through manual skill and straightforward deception. One useful example was provided for him by a contemporary juggler called Brandon. He had painted a picture of a dove on a wall, and, spying a pigeon on the roof of a house, had said to King Henry VIII 'Lo now your Grace shall we see what a iuggler can doo, if he be his craftes maister', and stabbed the picture several times – at which the pigeon had fallen dead to the ground. The king, horrified, had demanded that he never do such a thing again, for fear that the technique might be used to murder someone. The secret, Scot explained, was that the pigeon had beforehand been given a poison that would kill it within half an hour and had simply gone to sit next to another pigeon already on the house roof. Meanwhile 'the iuggler vseth words of art, partlie to protract the time, and partlie to gaine credit and admiration of the beholders', Scot continued, adding: 'If this or the like feate should be done by an old woman, euerie bodie would crie out, for fier and faggot to burne the witch.' Jugglers trod a fine line between spectacular entertainment and the sort of shock and fear that could lead them to danger.

Becoming respectable

One of the first magical performers to attain genuine respectability was Isaac Fawkes (d. 1731). He was careful to separate himself from those predecessors whose antics had caused consternation as fraudulent or devilish. He did not use fake familiars and on the whole tended not to draw attention, except ironically, to the possibility of demonic interventions. He described himself as an artist in 'dexterity of hand'. With an eye to the importance of status he repeatedly made it clear when publicising his shows that the royal family acted as his patrons. In his performances he settled for conventional clothing and wig rather than the juggler's traditional bright costume. His choice of tricks avoided the unpleasant or unsettling and tended towards the straightforwardly surprising: no decapitations, for instance, or piercing of the hands. While, like his predecessors, he performed at fairs, by the mid-eighteenth century they themselves were gaining at least a vestige of respectability; crucially, he also performed at fixed venues such as the Long Room in the Opera House at Haymarket and the Old Tennis Court in James Street, both in London, where he added machines (particularly automata), and included a 'freak show' element.

Indeed, through the eighteenth and nineteenth centuries, juggling was becoming stage magic – it was moving, in other words, into the theatre. Older forms persisted; towards the end of the eighteenth century a man known as 'Lane' (*fl.* 1778–1787) was performing at English fairs in the bright costumes of his predecessors. Nevertheless, by the mid-nineteenth century fairs were in decline. For magicians, this was balanced by their entry into other domains as 'polite' magic: not only theatres, but other public institutions and private clubs, from the American dime museums to London's Crystal Palace, which housed a permanent magic theatre around 1867–85. Individual performers shifted between settings and even styles of presentation, across the range of forums from fairs to theatres. Stage magic could also be combined with other pursuits entirely. In mainland Europe, Nicolas-Philippe Ledru (1731–1807), who travelled for many years as 'Comus', performed tricks and displayed electrical phenomena in the same shows; during the 1780s, despite the scorn of some learned contemporaries, Ledru achieved royal support to use his electrical expertise in the treatment of patients with nervous disorders. For most performers, however, sidelines were rather closer to home and usually had simple financial reasons. At around the time that Ledru was setting up his clinic, a former Italian professor of mathematics by the name of Giovanni Giuseppe Pinetti (1750–1800) was concluding a tour performing in Germany and moving to Paris himself – but he was forced to turn to writing rather than performing when in 1784 someone printed the secrets of his act. This was a danger to which itinerant jugglers were hardly exposed.

The rise of stage magic from the late eighteenth century into the nineteenth involved a shift that was intellectual as well as social and economic – specifically, it owed a great deal to performers' declared allegiance to what is today often referred to as the project of 'Enlightenment'. Just as touring lecturers sought to banish superstition in their audiences by using machines to demonstrate their rational, philosophical control over the effects of electricity and magnetism, so the new 'jugglers' of the eighteenth century used their skills – in such arts as legerdemain and misdirection – to reveal the tricks and subterfuge employed by those who claimed to possess genuine magical powers or display real spiritual phenomena. Through the great age of stage magic, performers emphasized their informed scepticism. The juggler's performance now represented (as one late-eighteenth-century writer remarked) 'a most agreeable antidote to superstition, and to that popular belief in miracles, exorcism, conjuration, sorcery, and witchcraft'.

Ventriloquism is an interesting example of this shift in emphasis. Having once been a minor element in the range of entertainments on offer during fairs and at markets, alongside such feats as juggling, music, and acrobatics, from the first quarter of the nineteenth century it emerged as a distinct act in stage performance. Its proponents could mimic people, animals, and other sounds, and could 'throw' their voices to make them seem to come from somewhere else. In these now rather familiar aspects of stage routine we can detect plays on earlier, more sinister beliefs – particularly the reproduction of noises and speech that might be devilish or divine. Jean-Baptiste de La Chapelle (*c*.1710–*c*.1792), the Parisian censor royal and a member of the Academies at Lyons and Rouen and the Royal Society of London, turned to a ventriloquist to help him demonstrate that with such skills it was straightforward to deceive people into thinking that they were observing supernatural phenomena.

Another case in point is the spread of so-called 'phantasmagoria', 'magic lantern' shows. The magic lantern used a bright light to project a still (but changeable) image onto a surface. The image could be altered or even made to move by, for instance, projecting it onto thick smoke. Popularized in Europe at the end of the eighteenth century by the Belgian performer Étienne Gaspard Robert ('Robertson', 1763–1837) and taken across the United States in the first quarter of the nineteenth century, such performances (in the words of an 1802 playbill) professed 'to expose the Practices of artful Impostors and pretended Exorcists, and to open the Eyes of those who still foster an absurd Belief in ghosts or disembodied spirits'; all of this would nevertheless 'afford also to the Spectator an interesting and pleasing entertainment'. The movement of performance magic from street to stage was a shift in respectability. Jugglers had been deceivers and con-artists who toyed with a reputation for calling on spirits; stage magicians were arch-rationalists who were open about their trickery and would reveal the secrets of the 'Impostors' who were not.

Stage magic

The nineteenth century was stage magic's heyday. Magical dynasties emerged: Compars Herrmann (1816–87) and his brother Alexander (1844–96), whose father had himself performed magic on stage, toured Europe then America together before choosing to continue separately. Alexander ('Herrmann the Great') spent time in London and Canada as well as mainland Europe before becoming an American citizen; in latter years he performed with his wife Adelaide (1853–1932), who continued with the act (and its bullet-catching trick) for more than a quarter of a century after his death. Leon Herrmann (1867–1909), the nephew of Compars and Alexander, pursued his own career in stage magic but found comparatively little success. The Herrmanns were not the only family of illusionists: the Bambergs in the Netherlands were involved in magic from the eighteenth century through to the twentieth. Eliaser Bamberg (1760–1833) performed in public spaces and in the homes of people who could pay; his son, David Leendart Bamberg (1786–1869), swapped this precarious existence for the position of court magician, a role into which *his* son (Tobias Bamberg, 1812–70) and grandson (David Tobias Bamberg, 1843–1914) followed. The forum for performance might change, the style and tricks could vary – the impetus to perform magic clearly did not.

Meanwhile, John Henry Anderson (1814–74), of Aberdeenshire in Scotland (one of several magicians associated around this time with a trick in which a live rabbit was removed from a hat), toured for most of his life as 'The Great Wizard of the North', performing in Europe, the United States, Canada, and Australia. In 1853, returning to London after a long tour, he encountered a rival drawing large crowds and fled back to Boston to work for a while before making the journey again. The man whose presence had prompted him to flee was the renowned French magician Jean-Eugène Robert-Houdin (1805–71). A former watchmaker, Robert-Houdin was fascinated by mechanisms and constructed automata and mechanical devices to produce stage effects. He was the magician at the

Palais-Royal in Paris from 1845 to 1855, and performed in Belgium and Germany during this period in addition to his visits to London. Like Fawkes, Robert-Houdin was known for wearing the same dress as his audience: he performed attired as a modern gentleman, not as an outlandish, exotic, or archaic mystery. Moreover, Robert-Houdin, like Anderson, divided his time between the theatres and private parties, not the marketplaces and fairs of his predecessors.

One of England's most influential magicians during the period after the heyday of Anderson and Robert-Houdin was John Nevil Maskelyne (1839–1917). After working for eight years on a touring show, he and his friend George Alfred Cooke (1825–1905) visited London and stayed, leasing a space at the Egyptian Hall in Piccadilly and running it as 'England's Home of Mystery'. When the lease ran out in 1904 they moved to St George's Hall, Langham Place. Cooke died the following year. His place in the partnership was taken by David Devant (1868–1941), a long-time admirer of Maskelyne's who had performed for Maskelyne and Cooke since 1893; together Devant and Maskelyne ran St George's Hall till 1915. The new partners were immediately active in an organization that emerged in 1905. After a meeting of twenty-three amateur and professional magicians at Pinoli's Restaurant in Wardour Street, London, the Magic Circle was founded as a society of illusionists. Devant was made the first president (though he resigned the role after a year because of the pressure of the work), Maskelyne edited the first issue of the society's periodical *The Magic Circular* in 1906, and meetings were held in a room at St George's Hall. In this, the British illusionists were following in the footsteps of the Society of American Magicians, founded late in 1902 in a New York magic shop to foster a sense of community among performers and protect the secrets of their trade.

By this point, magic had entered music-hall and vaudeville. It was during the second half of the nineteenth century that magicians began to employ young women as assistants on stage. Commercial concerns were driving performers towards greater novelty, whether in the tricks used or in where the shows took place. One of the most famous magicians ever to perform was, in 1899, embarking on a career that would take him outside the familiar venues. Erich Weiss (1874–1926), the son of a family of Hungarian immigrants living in New York, for a while worked hard performing card tricks in dime museums and sideshows; feats of escape (particularly from handcuffs) fascinated him, however, and under the guidance of a new manager, Martin Beck, he began from 1899 to focus on these. Selecting his stage name, Weiss turned to Robert-Houdin (whose deeds had so inspired him) and decided to become Harry Houdini. Touring Europe from 1900 he caused a sensation; at each place he stopped he would challenge local police to secure him however they could, in chains and in prisons, then he would escape. He returned to America in 1904 and for the next few years toured there, freeing himself from the increasingly outlandish traps devised by audience members. His primary stage was vaudeville: for most of his career he worked as the headline act (and highest paid performer) in vaudeville theatres across the United States. He also became influential within his genre, serving as president of the Society of American Magicians from 1917 until his death in 1926. He remains best known, however, for performances that ultimately outgrew the physical confines of the stage.

Rationalist magicians

Through the nineteenth century and beyond, magical performers of all kinds declared their continuing commitment to the rationalist project of uncovering the deception used by those who falsely claimed real magical and religious phenomena. One illusionist, William Pinchbeck, explained that his writing was 'not only to amuse and instruct, but also to convince superstition of her many ridiculous errors'. Superstitions were 'dangerous ... to society' and 'ruinous to the common interests of mankind.' P. T. Barnum (1810–91) wrote admiringly of a magician with whom he had toured the Southern States. This man had 'astonished his auditors with his deceptions', then later showed 'how each trick was performed, and how every man might thus become his own magician'. Barnum himself played throughout his career on the relationship between credulity and scepticism; he achieved renewed interest in a show he was running in the mid-1830s by claiming anonymously in a newspaper that its exhibit, Joice Heth, supposedly the 161-year-old nurse of George Washington, was actually an automaton voiced by a ventriloquist.

By the later nineteenth century, the key target for magicians' rationalist ire was spiritualism; psychical researchers investigating spiritualist phenomena tended to seek help from expert illusionists. Much attention through the middle years of the century focused on the American spiritual mediums Ira and William Davenport, who toured the world with a show that included phenomena such as banging noises and musical instruments being played in darkened rooms while the mediums were apparently tied up. Both the French performer Robert-Houdin and the Scottish magician John Henry Anderson denounced the Davenports, while P. T. Barnum called them 'impostors' and explained that he felt it was his duty to expose them because they were dishonest in their trickery. In 1909 a retired Ira Davenport (1839–1911) was visited by Houdini, who apparently listened to the medium's confession.

Houdini remained publicly silent on this meeting for over a decade; but through the 1920s, after his mother's death, he gained a reputation for exposing fraudulent spirit mediums. He attended séances, eventually disguising himself and bringing a reporter and a police officer in tow. In 1924 he revealed a

Boston medium known as 'Margery' (real name Mina Crandon) to be a fraud; from 1923 he was also a member of a *Scientific American* committee offering a cash prize to any medium able to demonstrate psychic abilities. Famously, Houdini's activities in this area caused a rift with Sir Arthur Conan Doyle, who spent his latter years seeking truth in the Spiritualism that Houdini so strongly criticized. Doyle concluded that Houdini was himself a powerful spirit medium who had used his abilities during his stage career and was now employing them to thwart the performers he claimed to be exposing as frauds.

The English illusionist J. N. Maskelyne, who became one of England's foremost opponents of spiritualism, began his career by confronting the Davenports. He had served an apprenticeship as a watchmaker, but his amateur interest in conjuring saw him selected to attend a séance at Cheltenham Town Hall in 1865 in order to test the Davenports' claims. Unimpressed, Maskelyne vowed to demonstrate that their feats could be achieved through practice and ingenuity. A couple of months later he and his friend Cooke began working as (in the words of their playbill) 'the only successful rivals of the Davenport Brothers ... showing the possibility of accomplishing, without the aid of spiritualism, not only all the Davenports' tricks, but many others, original and more astounding'. They gained enough publicity to tour as performers, and Maskelyne was pleased enough with the outcome that he began a lifelong campaign against the false claims made by spiritualists. Even Maskelyne's subsequent role as theatre manager did not dull his crusading spirit: performers who claimed the ability to conjure spirits were barred from performing at his venues.

Spirit mediums were not the only people claiming that their feats were down to genuine powers rather than trickery or sleight of hand. To Maskelyne's annoyance, a growing genre of show in the latter part of the nineteenth century was that of the 'mentalist' performer – people who claimed to be able to read

HARRY KELLAR WRITES ON SLATE

Harry Kellar (1849–1922), performing in Philadelphia in 1885, exposed the trickery of the medium Dr Henry Slade (c. 1835–1905), famed for displays in which spirits apparently wrote on slates; he reproduced the *Philadelphia Report*'s account in *A Magician's Tour* (1886). 'Mr Kellar's object was to demonstrate that he could produce by natural agencies what Dr Slade professes to accomplish by spiritualism.' Kellar, seated with his audience at a table, washed nine slates and chose two; 'then placing a piece of pencil between them he held them aloft in full sight of everyone present. Immediately a scratching sound was heard'; the slates now bore the message: 'It would perhaps be easier to believe that these manifestations are the result of spiritual power, than that they are merely a conjurer's trick. They can, however, all be traced to natural causes.' Further slates were produced with various messages. Finally, an audience member wrote on a slate the question 'What is the height of the Washington Monument?' without showing Kellar, and placed it under the table. More scratching, and now on the slate's other side it read: 'We have never visited the Washington Monument, therefore can not give its height.'

minds. One such was Washington Irving Bishop (1856–1889), an American performer who began his career in 1876 by exposing the methods of his former associate, the stage spiritualist Anna Eva Fay (Annie Pingree, c.1851–1927). A year later he added mind-reading to his repertoire, and in the next few years became famous for it. He claimed no supernatural powers, but rather receptivity to others' mental activity. This domain, encompassing performers of various kinds from hypnotists to clairvoyants, would in due course be called the 'paranormal', and reading minds 'telepathy'.

Many of the more traditional stage magicians remained highly doubtful, and on tour in England, Bishop was challenged by Henry Labouchère (1831–1912), the editor of a weekly journal called *Truth*, to a bet over whether Bishop could identify the serial number on a banknote sealed in an envelope; though the offer was withdrawn when they failed to agree on the assistant, Bishop successfully listed the numbers at a performance at St James Hall, and went on to attack Labouchère in print, along with those he saw as critics in league with him. He accused Maskelyne of conspiring with the journalist, calling him 'a man devoid of honourable instincts' and threatening to hold him 'criminally liable and make justice punish him heavily for his villainous conduct'. Maskelyne sued and won, but Bishop returned to the United States and Maskelyne never received his money.

As Simon During has pointed out, the dispute was as much as anything about divergent approaches to magic as entertainment. They differed over where magic was done, the kinds of things it might consist in, and the role of print. Maskelyne's shows were based in the theatres and other established institutions, and they employed impressive mechanisms and machines to create their effects; Maskelyne produced advertisements to encourage people to visit his shows. Bishop performed in many other spaces, often public ones, and he took great care managing publicity and tailoring his performances to increase his fame. His tricks involved apparent feats of the mind, not large-scale mechanical contraptions, and he claimed genuine powers.

Maskelyne, for his part, remained committed to stage magic as a rational force. He pursued his campaign into the Magic Circle as one of its founder members. The organization included some whose primary interest was investigation into occult phenomena: the Director of the National Laboratory for Psychical Science, Harry Price (1881–1948), joined in 1920. In 1914, however, Maskelyne went further and established an 'Occult Committee' within the Magic Circle specifically to investigate claims to supernatural powers – especially claims of the kind made by spiritualist mediums. At that point he had recently authored an attack on the spirit medium Madame Blavatsky and her Theosophical Society, under the conciliatory title *The Fraud of Modern Theosophy Exposed: a Brief History of the Greatest Imposture ever Perpetrated under the Cloak of Religion.*

He had also published an explanation for the mysterious 'Indian rope trick' that had preoccupied Western commentators for decades: the magician throws one end of a rope into the air, where it stays, rigid and vertical; then a boy climbs up the rope and disappears. Maskelyne suggested that the rope had bamboo segments to help it stand upright. It was not the right explanation – as Peter Lamont has masterfully demonstrated in a recent book, the Indian rope trick in the form we know it was never actually performed – but Maskelyne was only one of many illusionists proffering explanations for the impressive feat. In 1933, long after Maskelyne's death, his Occult Committee was reappointed to return to the topic. They concluded that the supposed trick was actually a hoax that no one had truly seen, but in a twist whose irony may well have been lost on committee members, the legend proved too attractive to let go of and the real explanation was largely ignored for decades.

Screen magic

Though the magic lantern played a central role in many illusions produced in shows throughout the nineteenth century, it only came to public attention in the last decades before 1900; so it remained a secret and impressive weapon in the magician's armoury. Sometimes it was used in a relatively straightforward way: in Robertson's *Fantasmagorie* apparitions were produced by projecting images onto smoke, which made them appear to shift and change. Exactly the same technique could be used in other tricks, however: many of the acts in which people were burned alive on stage (then resurrected) probably involved a carefully managed switch from the plain sight of the apparent victim, enveloped in smoke, to a projection onto that smoke. Nonetheless, the images produced were still; it was in 1894 with Thomas Edison's creation of the 'Kinetoscope', which permitted 'living pictures' within a peepshow format, that creating a moving, projected image (by combining the two devices) became a realistic possibility. The worldwide race to achieve this was won by Louis Lumière, who first demonstrated his 'Cinématographe' at the Grand Café in Paris in December 1895 and sent representatives across the world, but his competitors were close behind.

Shows at the Egyptian Hall in London used lanterns to project images which helped create scenes within which the 'magic' would take place. As at other venues across Europe, other devices were employed to create optical illusions. The use of this machinery and little-known scientific developments was well established in stage magic. David Devant, Maskelyne's future partner, was by this point one of Egyptian Hall's most important performers. He was, among other things, a renowned shadowgraphist: he used the light cast by a magic lantern to act out dramatic sequences in silhouette using his hands and props to make shadow puppets. Early in 1896 Devant attended previews of the mysterious new device at the Polytechnic in London; though he immediately wanted one, the cost of hiring was so high that instead he bought outright an alternative machine produced by the English optical instrument maker R. W. Paul. By the end of March Devant was using the machine in his act, while Paul himself began filming Devant's tricks and replaying them around the country.

The Théâtre Robert-Houdin in Paris, which had continued to put on magic shows for more than seventy years since its foundation in 1845 by Robert-Houdin himself, was led into showing films by Marie-Georges-Jean Méliès (1861–1938).

Méliès, inspired by the experience of visiting shows at the Egyptian Hall, had sold his share of the family shoe business to buy the Théâtre Robert-Houdin in 1888 and reverse its decline. He used scenery and lantern projections to build up fantastic settings for stories; these scenes could be changed to represent (for instance) the passage of time or violent changes in the weather. He was present at Lumière's demonstration of the first Cinématographe in Paris at the end of 1895. Like Devant, he tried to buy a projector and was rebuffed (and quoted an extortionate price for hiring); like Devant he turned to Paul's machine. He called it the Méliès Kinétograph and devised his own camera to capture moving images. His films used simple techniques to achieve striking visual effects – such as making an item disappear by stopping the camera briefly to remove it from shot.

A number of magicians took to the new technology. Carl Hertz (1859–1924), an American illusionist, was the first to bring it to Australia while on tour, beating even the employee of Lumière's sent there with a Cinématographe; he made a considerable profit, but the films he showed began to eclipse his magic performances. Alexander Victor (1878–1961), a Swedish magician who toured as 'Alexander the Great', eventually achieved success in the United States with a projector for use at home. Harry Houdini himself, having in 1901 taken part in a Pathé film that demonstrated some of his most famous escapes, was consulted as a technical expert by the same company to help produce special effects for *The Mysteries of Myra* in 1906. In later years – notably from 1918 until 1923 – he took part in a series of films as actor and, later, producer; his brother, Theodore Hardeen (1876–1945), temporarily gave up his own career as a stage magician to join Houdini in the film business. Altogether Houdini lost half a million dollars in the venture.

As the shifts of personnel from stage to screen (or in front of the curtain to behind the camera) hint, a broader trend was at work: cinemas were drawing audiences away from theatres – and stage magic in particular was being eclipsed by the magic of film. With tastes shifting towards longer presentations and attractive performers acting out dramatic and romantic plots, the work was increasingly carried out by large companies. When Houdini visited the Théâtre Robert-Houdin in 1901 he was dismayed to discover that stage magicians had been relegated to the afternoons, replaced in the evenings by cinema. Méliès made no films after 1913; he returned briefly to performing at Robert-Houdin, but he gave his last performance there in 1920 and it was demolished not long afterwards. St George's Hall in London ('England's Home of Mystery' after Egyptian Hall) had become a cinema by 1926; later still it was being used by the BBC. By the mid-1920s, magic theatres had disappeared from the landscape, changed into cinemas or closed down.

Although films plotted to include magical deeds continued to draw audiences for a century after the introduction of the Cinématographe, and beyond, most pernicious was the use of 'special effects' in films where magic and illusion were not of prime interest. Méliès himself saw this change and denounced it. He equated the image on film with the unchanging, framed view audiences enjoyed in the theatre; other directors were jumping from one camera position to another, dissolving one scene into another, or even using close-up shots that rendered things (often parts of people's bodies) suddenly colossal. These, in the view of Méliès, were magic tricks, but peculiar ones – tricks that were employed unannounced. This was magic that he found confusing rather than spectacular. Interestingly, the word 'magic' is still used to describe cinema and special effects in particular, from the phrase 'movie magic' to the name of the company established in 1975 by George Lucas to provide effects for his film *Star Wars*: Industrial Light and Magic. Magic has largely become removed from film; though the technology had originally found its most natural home in the stage acts of conjurors, and though the techniques employed were recognized by illusionists as being undeclared illusions, it has ceased to be wonderful, and ceased to seem illusory. We now watch wildlife documentaries without considering slow-motion or stop-motion camerawork as being in any way a conjuring trick.

The impact of the new visual media on stage magic was felt for several decades. The United States in particular saw a downturn in the popularity of conjuring in the middle years of the twentieth century, with its revival credited to performers such as Doug Henning (1947–2000), whose 1970s series *Doug Henning's World of Magic* drew impressive audiences and award nominations. Live audiences have become as important to television programmes as they were in the theatre, if only to reassure viewers that there has been no alteration to the footage between recording and broadcast – no 'camera trickery', to use the familiar phrase. Mark Wilson (b. 1929), pioneer of televised magic, responded to doubts about how successful it would be by establishing in 1960 a formula that has governed much shown since: programmes would be recorded before an audience, whose view the camera would clearly replicate – without cutting from one point of view to another mid-trick. The audiences used in the years since have ranged from seated groups, as if watching a theatrical performance, to the individual witnesses of 'close up' work, such as card tricks. In 1997, David Blaine (b. 1973) was lauded for his programme *Street Magic*, in which he roved city streets in America, performing illusions for those he met, the camerawork handheld in *reportage* style and the chance personal encounters squarely at the programme's heart.

For all the changes invited and demanded by the technology of recording and broadcast, there were constants. One was the persistent ambivalence of illusionists' role: at its heart, stage magic is about deception, but stage magicians often spend much of their time uncovering the deceptions of others. The 'Amazing Randi' (born in 1929 as Randall James Hamilton Zwinge) combined his successful career as a conjuror with a campaign to challenge those claiming paranormal or supernatural powers, and since his retirement has concentrated entirely on these investigations. He was a founding fellow of the Committee for Scientific Investigation of Claims of the Paranormal. Inspired by Randi, Penn & Teller (Penn Fraser Jillette, b. 1955, and Teller, born Raymond Joseph Teller in 1948) have more recently focused attention on psychics, the paranormal, and other favourite targets, alongside their continuing, highly successful conjuring career. In Britain, Derren Brown (b. 1971) has not only combined stage magic techniques with suggestion and misdirection to produce a modern take on the 'mind reading' show, he has also confronted paranormal and supernatural claims and our susceptibility to them. In 2004, in a programme whose principles might be familiar to the 'Enlightened' magicians of the eighteenth century, he held a séance in which he convinced a group of participants that they were communicating with the spirit of a woman who had committed suicide in the room thirty years previously – before uncovering his deception and explaining the methods he had used. Still more recently he has explored his interest in the manipulation of people, convincing a group signed up to a 'motivational seminar' to rob a security van without directly instructing them or even explicitly prompting the idea. Brown has been criticized for his claims to be engaging in subtle psychological manipulation by those who suggest that the effects are often achieved employing traditional techniques of stage magic; his response is to point out that he may be dishonest in his performances but is 'always honest' about his dishonesty. Such playfulness over the magician's role as guardian of rationality may be disquieting but it has a long history.

One of the world's best known and most controversial performers in recent years has been David Blaine, who followed up *Street Magic* with a series of endurance stunts whose status is still debated. He has, among other things, been buried, encased in ice, submerged in water, and attached to a spinning gyroscope. His self-portrayal is as heir to Houdini's tradition of impressive physical feats; escapology with fewer escapes. It is also possible to see his performances as echoes of older forms: in medieval parlance, illusions were 'feats of activity', an umbrella term also taking in displays of acrobatics or balance; the Indian fakirs who occasioned much discussion in the nineteenth century (and to whom I will return in the last chapter) were known for their supposed ability to overcome serious physical deprivation (as well as, for instance, levitating and recovering from decapitation). Nonetheless, critics including Penn Jillette have remained unimpressed, pointing out that Blaine's deeds are difficult but not mysterious, and not difficult enough to be mysterious. (There may be echoes here of the clash of cultures between John Nevil Maskelyne and Washington Irving Bishop, between the traditional magic of the theatre and the magic of crowds in public spaces and press releases.) Whatever the truth of it, and however we choose to position Blaine's stunts with respect to the art of conjuring, the focus of these performers and their debates remains the boundaries of what is physically possible and what must be illusory; and the aim of their performances is still spectacle.

4

The occult

Magic in modern times has largely been about ritual. Over the course of two millennia magic had shifted from a suspect and possibly devilish pursuit, attacking by subterfuge and corroding Christian society, to a philosophy of nature whose practitioners were just a little less than divine, and had finally become the refuge of the unlearned and unwise. The magician of the later eighteenth century was the magician as trickster, perhaps demonstrating the impostures of those who stood in the way of Enlightenment, but often simply a street performer, tarnished as a con-artist. The Enlightenment magician was rationalist but untrustworthy. Through the nineteenth and twentieth centuries, however, a new way of understanding magic gained popularity, embraced by a succession of individuals and groups reacting to the predominant values of the post-Enlightenment West. Magic provided something to reach for beyond the rational, scientific view of the world. Modern practitioners increasingly separated magic from its previous Christian framework; instead, they saw it as transcending or even replacing Christianity, looking back to pagan origins or a deeper unity of religious doctrines. This chapter examines modern magic.

Freemasons and Rosicrucians

Through the eighteenth century there is little extant evidence of a tradition of learned magic. As chapter 1 explained, cunning folk continued to engage in the same magical and divinatory practices that they had for centuries, through into the nineteenth century;

but we have few documents discussing magical theory. What the age of Enlightenment did have was secret societies. Groups of Freemasons and Rosicrucians constructed their initiation rituals and other ceremonies around the symbolism of learned magic without actually encouraging its practice. The Rosicrucians, or Fraternity of the Rosy Cross, had first been mentioned in three works published in Cassel (Germany) between 1614 and 1616; then in 1623 notices appeared across Paris announcing the Rosicrucians' presence there – and causing considerable excitement. From these various documents it was possible to build up a picture of the mysterious Fraternity. They claimed that it had been founded by a 'Father C.R.C.', usually identified with 'Christian Rosencreutz' (the subject of the third German publication); he had been born in 1375 and had lived for 106 years. 'Father C.R.C.' had travelled in the East and learned all there was to know from sages there. His Fellowship were to wear the clothes of their countrymen (not don special outfits), would meet annually, and were to heal the sick for free. The actual history of the Rosicrucians is hard to establish, though recent scholarship has suggested that the Parisian episode at least was a hoax.

Whatever the truth of their origins, by the eighteenth century there were groups claiming descent from this secret society of adepts. A group of Freemasons called the Ancient and Accepted Rite drew on the pamphlets for the rite of admission to their eighteenth degree, 'the Rose Croix'. Across continental Europe and in England these groups flourished, to the consternation of social and religious conservatives, who, by the end of the eighteenth century had begun to conceive of Freemasonry as a radical international conspiracy and link it to the French Revolution. One author even claimed that they had inherited the task of undermining Christian society from a chain of other secret groups stretching back to the time of Christ himself. These mysterious organizations included Gnostics, the Cathars, and the Knights Templar. The survival of this peculiar myth was ensured by the reaction of the revolutionaries with whom Freemasonry had become associated; they embraced it. Yes (they agreed), the Gnostics, Cathars, Templars, and Freemasons were connected; they all possessed knowledge that could overturn the orthodox view of Christianity and the reactionary politics that it upheld. It is an account that has proved remarkably tenacious.

An early precursor of the 'occult revival' that eventually took shape in nineteenth-century Europe was written by an English author, Francis Barrett (*fl.* 1780–1814), who claimed on its frontispiece to be a 'Brother of the Rose Cross' (*Frater rosae crucis*). The book, published in 1801, was *The Magus, or, Celestial Intelligencer*. In this work Barrett had compiled English translations of medieval and early modern magical and alchemical works, covering topics from natural magic and alchemy through to the use of talismans, number magic, and the lives of famous adepts. He also included portraits of the demons that practitioners of ritual magic could conjure. Barrett used the work to advertise instruction in 'the choicest operations of Natural Philosophy, Natural Magic, the Cabbala, Chemistry, the Talismanic Arts, Hermetic Philosophy, Astrology, Physiognomy, etc., etc.', and promised to provide 'the knowledge of the Rites, Mysteries, Ceremonies and Principles of the ancient Philosophers, Magi, Cabbalists, and Adepts'. Barrett's successors had little regard for his work. A. E. Waite called him a 'credulous amateur' and Aleister Crowley pointed out that *The Magus* consisted largely of extracts from Agrippa's *Three Books of Occult Philosophy*. Notwithstanding all this, Barrett's book could boast one important reader – a Frenchman who would influence the practice of magic well into the twentieth century: Éliphas Lévi.

Éliphas Lévi

It was in France that the revival of magic truly began, and one of its key figures was Alphonse Louis Constant (1810–75), a shoemaker's son in post-Revolutionary Paris who had attended a seminary but left without being ordained as a priest. Constant's interest in magic and related topics helped him make ends meet: he gave lessons on them to supplement his slight journalistic income. In May 1854, after the end of his marriage, he travelled to England to draw on his burgeoning reputation as an expert in magic to earn more money giving lessons there, but his lack of English stymied him and he was dismayed to find himself chiefly in demand putting on demonstrations of ritual magic. Constant had arrived in England with letters of introduction, and he made friends rapidly with one recipient, Edward Bulwer Lytton (1803–73), a politician and the author of a novel about Rosicrucianism. Lytton encouraged Constant to write a book on magic; the result, in 1855, was *Dogme et rituel de la haute magie* (*Dogma and Ritual of High Magic*), produced under a pseudonym which was an attempt to render his given names in Hebrew: Éliphas Lévi. Defeated by his financial situation, he had by this time returned to Paris with no money and no home, to take refuge at a friend's house; now, finally, his fame drew to him students who spoke his language and who were keen to learn about the cabbala. He continued to write books on magic, but by the time he died in 1875, he had reconciled with the Catholic Church and taken the last rites.

Lévi's cosmology and his magical system were a blend of medieval and early modern magic and alchemy with recent philosophy. He linked his ideas to historical authors and groups to claim that they had a long history – making them seem more reliable than if he had acknowledged that they were his. In short, he presented his work as ancient wisdom. Moreover, he came up with a term to describe this mysterious tradition: 'occultism'. Previously, 'occult' had been an adjective – people had referred to occult philosophies or occult sciences, occult properties, occult qualities, occult forces; henceforth they would refer to 'occultists', 'occultism', and 'the occult'.

Lévi's blending of disparate traditions into one was far from atypical, but it was influential. The first sentence of his *Dogme et rituel* explained his underlying picture:

> Behind the veil of all the hieratic and mystical allegories of ancient doctrines, behind the darkness and strange ordeals of all initiations, under the seal of all sacred writings, in the ruins of Nineveh or Thebes, on the crumbling stones of old temples and on the blackened visage of the Assyrian or Egyptian sphinx, in the monstrous or marvellous paintings which interpret to the faithful of India the inspired pages of the Vedas, in the cryptic emblems of our old books on alchemy, in the ceremonies practised at reception by all secret societies, there are found indications of a doctrine which is everywhere the same and everywhere carefully concealed.

The root problem was that the powers and knowledge with which mankind had originally been entrusted had been lost outside these secret societies; they were recoverable through study and by practice – activities for which Lévi was providing the basis.

In *Dogme et rituel*, Lévi explained that the world was suffused with a fluid that permeated all things, what he called the 'astral light'; it was the medium that held all ideas, images, and details of everything that had ever existed or happened; these could be seen by the mind's eye, the imagination, and controlled by the will. Likenesses could be called up out of the astral light and presented to the senses. This, he explained, was how necromancy – consulting with the dead – worked. 'It is by means of this light', he noted, 'that static visionaries place themselves in communication with all worlds'. Astral light acted directly on the nerves, and Lévi linked it directly with what Anton Mesmer had called 'animal magnetism' a half century earlier – a type of magnetism associated with living things and susceptible to control by skilled practitioners who could generate trance states in their patients. For Lévi, all such phenomena reflected the effects of astral light, and the magus achieved his wonderful deeds through willpower.

Even in circumstances where spirits apparently participated, it was often simply a case of impressions being called up from the astral light. Lévi reported that on his first English trip he had been asked to summon Apollonius of Tyana a first-century sage posthumously renowned as a magician. After three weeks of preparation by restricting himself to a vegetarian diet then by fasting, while meditating on Apollonius, he had performed a twelve-hour ritual in a 'temple' containing four concave mirrors and an altar. Enrobed in white and carrying a sword, he had chanted until a figure in a shroud appeared briefly; something had touched his arm whereupon it had gone numb, then the figure had reappeared and he had fainted. In his account of the episode Lévi explained that the effect of his preparations and the sights and smells of the ritual had been 'an actual drunkenness of the imagination', and insisted only that he really had seen and touched as he described. There was, in the last analysis, 'no proof whatsoever that spirits leave the higher spheres to communicate with us'; rather, such ceremonies 'evoke the memories which they have left in the Astral Light'. These were echoes of the live people, not messages from their immortal souls.

This was not to say that people did not actually deal with spirits. Lévi took great care to explain that the pentagram (a five-pointed star) 'signifies the domination of the mind over the elements, and the demons of the air, the spirits of fire, the phantoms of water and ghosts of earth are enchained by this sign'. The magus who employed it would 'be ministered unto by legions of angels and hosts of fiends'. Existing lore held that spirits could be warded off or driven away using the pentagram; Lévi extended this to explain that as they could be trapped in a pentagram drawn within a circle, they could be forced to appear there too. In other words, the pentagram could be used to conjure up as well as to banish. It was powerful, he explained, because it represented the will's rule over the astral light; but its power was dependent on the wisdom of the person who employed it – the spirits concerned were sensitive to whether it was 'employed with understanding' or not. Those who tried to use it to invoke spirits and failed were simply demonstrating their ignorance. Lévi also distinguished two different meanings for the pentagram, according to whether two of its five points were angled downwards or only one. If two pointed down, it symbolized God; if only one, then the Devil. Both combined (the second inside the first) signified the Holy Spirit.

Crucial to Lévi's magical system was the tarot. Since the medieval period tarot decks had been used for card games: they consist of four suits, each of fourteen cards, plus a suit of twenty-one trumps ('tarots') and an extra trump called the 'Fool'. In the late eighteenth century diviners began to employ the tarot deck, and particularly its twenty-two trumps (or 'Arcana major' as they called them). Antoine Court de Gébelin (d. 1784), a Swiss clergyman and Freemason, had claimed in 1781 that the symbolism used was connected to the Egyptian gods Isis and Thoth; Lévi stressed a link with the Hebrew tradition. 'The absolute kabalistic alphabet', he wrote, 'was then called the Key of Solomon.' He further argued that 'these Keys, preserved to our own day, but wholly misconstrued, are nothing else than the game of Tarot, the antique allegories of which were remarked and appreciated for the first time in the modern world by the learned archaeologist, Court de Gébelin'. The tarot was 'the primeval book and the keystone of the occult sciences'. The 'most perfect instrument of divination', it was a 'miraculous work which inspired all the sacred books of antiquity'; its twenty-two arcana were linked to letters of the Hebrew alphabet and thus to cabbalistic teachings. In fact, *Dogme et rituel* itself was divided into two parts, each consisting of twenty-two chapters, the chapters corresponding to the tarot arcana. The images of the tarot arcana were magical symbols ('pentacles'), which expressed a doctrine and served 'to focus all intellectual force into a glance, a recollection, a touch'. It was, he explained, 'a starting-point for the efficient projection of will'. The practitioner was to concentrate on one of these symbols as a way of preparing the mind for magic.

Lévi used one particular arcanum image as the frontispiece for the second volume of *Dogme et rituel*: number fifteen, depicting 'a monster throned upon an altar, mitred and horned, having a woman's breasts and the generative organs of a man – a chimera, a malformed sphinx, a synthesis of deformities'. This figure, labelled 'THE DEVIL' in the tarot (and reproduced here as figure 4), he identified with 'the Baphomet of the Templars', the idol that certain Knights Templar had supposedly confessed under torture to worshipping. Some had said that it was a disembodied head; others, he explained, described it as 'a demon in the form of a goat'. Figures with similar characteristics had been discovered elsewhere: Lévi pointed particularly to the 'Goat of Mendes', an Egyptian god reported by Herodotus. He insisted that the Templars really had worshipped this goat-headed figure, but stressed that it did not represent the devil but rather Pan, whom he called 'the god of our modern schools of philosophy'. He went through the image's symbolism, from the upright pentagram on the figure's forehead (a good sign) to the pointing arms, to the 'torch of intelligence burning between the horns'. The caduceus (staff encircled by two serpents) in its lap represented eternal life, while humanity was depicted in its androgynous physical characteristics. The scales on its belly, the ring round the caduceus, the writing on its arms; all had symbolic implications. In Lévi's own cabbalistic/astrological tarot system, this image was associated with the Hebrew character ס (samekh), and the 'Heaven of Mercury'.

Successive writers on the subject would rework the system of correspondences associating cabbala, tarot, and the heavens. They would draw on Lévi's writings but forge new rituals and

Figure 4 Éliphas Lévi's image of the 'goat of Mendes', or Baphomet, supposedly worshipped by the Knights Templar

practices. Particularly influential, in this and in other matters, were the teachings of a group established in England in the latter years of the nineteenth century.

The Hermetic Order of the Golden Dawn

Fact and legend are tricky to disentangle in accounts of the organization's origins. According to a later tradition, a coroner in London, Dr William Wynn Westcott (1848–1925), was given an interesting manuscript in 1887 by a fellow Freemason and occultist, the Reverend Alphonsus F. A. Woodford. Woodford claimed that the manuscript, which was in cipher, would illuminate Rosicrucian secrets; Westcott found in the decoded piece references to 'Fratres' and 'Sorores', a 'grade of Neophyte', and a Temple of the 'Golden Dawn'. It contained details of initiation rituals to five grades of a mysterious order and some associated teachings concerning ritual magic, including cabbala and Egyptian materials. Intrigued, Westcott turned to another Freemason and occultist (and self-proclaimed Scottish nobleman), Samuel Liddell (MacGregor) Mathers (1854–1918), to help turn the documents into the basis for a new organization. Westcott also uncovered in the writings the details of a high Rosicrucian adept in Germany, Anna Sprengel of Nuremberg, later known to them as 'Soror Sapiens Dominabitur Astris' ('The Wise Sister Will Rule Over the Stars'). He reported to the others her permission to establish an English branch of the German Order 'Die Goldene Dämmerung' ('The Golden Dawn'), and signed a charter on her behalf. The two recruited a third Freemason, Dr William Robert Woodman (1828–91), and in 1888 in London set up the Isis-Urania Temple of the Hermetic Order of the Golden Dawn; before long an Osiris Temple was founded in Weston-super-Mare, a Horus Temple in Bradford, and an Amen-Ra Temple in Edinburgh. Woodman played little role in the society and died late in 1891; Westcott also reported Sprengel's death. Now he and Mathers continued by themselves, Mathers putting together rituals and compiling training documents. Members of the group would undergo instruction and undertake studies in the secret workings of the cosmos and in occult doctrines; they would also take part in rituals.

Under Lévi's influence, the eighteenth-century emphasis on Freemasonry had given way to the study of occultism; the Golden Dawn's founders had all been members of other groups. All three were Freemasons, and all three were members of the Societas Rosicruciana in Anglia, dedicated to the study of secret wisdom from past ages. Supposedly partly based on a late eighteenth-century German Masonic order, the Order of the Gold and Rosy Cross, the Rosicrucian Society in England had been set up in 1866 by Robert Wentworth Little, a young Freemason, with the aid of the occultist Kenneth Mackenzie. Mackenzie claimed not only to have visited Éliphas Lévi, but to have been initiated into a German 'Order of the Gold and Rosy Cross' – a group whose structure was reflected in the Societas Rosicruciana and in the documents passed on by the Reverend Woodford. Only Master Masons could join the Societas, and the Golden Dawn founders were all key members. Mackenzie himself knew Mathers and was one of the Golden Dawn's early recruits. Perhaps as important as Rosicrucianism was 'Hermeticism'; Westcott and Mathers were members of a short-lived group called the Hermetic Society. This concerned itself with 'Esoteric Christianity' – specifically, the idea that the gospels were allegorical rather than biographical, explaining the search for spiritual perfection rather than telling the story of a man's life. Christianity, they held, was not only consonant with earlier pagan wisdom, but was essentially an interpretation of it – and specifically of the wisdom contained within the Hermetic texts. The Hermetic Society dissolved in 1888 after its founder's death, the same year as the foundation of the first temples of the Hermetic Order of the Golden Dawn. Westcott was also a member of the Theosophical Society, an occult group established by the medium Madame Blavatsky. Despite the

'Neophyte' was added at the bottom of the hierarchy, numbered zero, for those who had just joined, and the remaining grades were divided into three orders, a First (Outer) Order and a Second (Inner) Order, along with a Third Order that was realistically out of reach of mortals. Those initiated into the Outer Order as Neophytes were sworn to secrecy and took a motto (usually in Latin) as a name; they then studied to rise up through the grades. Candidates often approached the order having participated in spiritualism; one of the first statements they were asked to sign on admission informed them that such activities as mesmerism and mediumship were disavowed by the order as they involved passivity of will, which the Golden Dawn rejected. The Neophyte ritual was based around the journey from darkness to light, its symbolism explained during the ceremony. Each new member was given a document that listed previous adepts claimed by the Order, including (for instance) Éliphas Lévi, and discussed its historical roots in ancient Egyptian wisdom and the Rosicrucians. Neophytes would, it assured, be taught 'the principles of Occult Science and the Magic of Hermes'. Candidates were initiated into a grade before being given any information about it, and instruction in that grade followed initiation. Each person progressed by taking exams. In the First Order, the subjects to be mastered included the symbolism used in astrological and alchemical texts; divination by geomancy and the tarot; the Hebrew alphabet; the cabbalistic Tree of Life; and more generally the esoteric traditions of societies from ancient Egypt to the early modern period. Each of the founders, uniquely, took on two grades; they became the visible 'Chiefs' of the First Order, who clearly ran it; and, under a different motto/name, they became more senior representatives of the 'Secret Chiefs' who ran the Second Order from behind the scenes. Westcott was 'Sapere Aude' ('Dare to Know') in one role and 'Non Omnia Moriar' ('Not All of Me Will Die') in the other. Members of the First Order were not told the identity of these higher officials; when they joined the Second Order and discovered that Westcott and Mathers were also fulfilling this role, they seem to have accepted that the men were acting on behalf of the invisible members of the Third Order. Mathers in particular claimed to be given constant guidance by these inhabitants of the astral plane in running the group.

The Second Order was established in 1892, when Mathers returned from a trip to Paris with a document that he explained had been given to him by a 'Frater L. E. T., a Continental Adept', specifying a new ritual. The Second Order he founded was known as the Ordo Rosae Rubeae et Aureae Crucis (R. R. et A. C., the Order of the Red Rose and Gold Cross). It was secret and selective even within the Golden Dawn; candidates were approached, and members of the First Order not approached remained ignorant of its existence. Its purpose was to train members in the practice of ritual magic. Those who joined it underwent the 'Portal ritual', whose symbolism referred to the legend of Christian Rosencreutz, purported founder of the original Rosicrucian group; the rite took place on new premises in a specially constructed symbolically decorated seven-sided chamber (the 'Vault') containing a coffin. In due course the administration and everyday running of the order were handed over to a Council of Adepts. Teaching consisted of lectures, many given by Mathers and Westcott and many preserved in manuscripts for future use. Yeats was one of the handful of people who entered this Second Order in its first year. Those who were fortunate enough to be approached were expected to demonstrate unimpeachable self-discipline and 'Purity of aspiration and of life' as well as technical mastery and wisdom. This was what the order meant by 'adept'.

For much of the Golden Dawn's existence, however, its founders and members were in dispute. In 1892 Mathers and his wife moved to Paris, relying on and falling out with successive representatives in London – first Annie Horniman, who became fed up with bankrolling them, then her successor, Florence Farr, who simply wished to give up her office to study with Westcott (he had stepped down in 1897 after a warning that his involvement was unbecoming of a coroner). Infuriated with Farr, Mathers lashed out at Westcott, accusing him of forging foundation documents (which had since disappeared); this started a chain of events that led the Second Order and the Isis-Urania Temple to break officially from Mathers in 1900.

Then late in 1901, a scandal erupted. A couple who had deceived Mathers about their occult credentials for just long enough to steal papers from him had used those documents to set up their own magical order when prevented from joining the Golden Dawn; now the husband was arrested for raping a sixteen-year-old girl who had become involved in his group. In court, the Golden Dawn's oaths and rituals (which had been copied by the defendants) were exposed to sustained and embarrassing scrutiny, and declared to be blasphemous. However slight the link, and however false the implication that the Golden Dawn was involved, the effect was immediate. First Order membership dropped promptly and seriously, and in June 1902 a new leadership introduced a new name: henceforth it would be the Hermetic Society of the M. R. (Morgenröthe, 'Dawn'). The Second Order suffered much less but had by now lost many of its longest standing and most senior members anyway. Further splits followed as the groups splintered into a multitude of societies all claiming to be the true inheritors of the Golden Dawn legacy, from A. E. Waite's Independent and Rectified Order Rosae Rubeae et Aureae Crucis to the new Mathers' order Alpha and Omega. In these years disciples also reached the United States and New Zealand; offshoots of the original order have remained active across the world in the decades since. Mathers died in 1918.

The Golden Dawn's magic

In the name of the order as a whole, the Golden Dawn tied itself to Hermeticism; in the name of its Second Order, it claimed a link to Rosicrucians. Golden Dawn initiates worked with Hermetic texts and practised the cabbala; its founders combined a diverse collection of materials and sources to create their magical system. The manuscript on which the order had been established referred to Egypt, and it was considered a major source; Neophytes were instructed that Rosicrucianism was indebted to Egyptian magic. Above all, however, Golden Dawn magic was a product of more recent writers, in particular Éliphas Lévi.

The Golden Dawn adapted Lévi's teaching on astral light. One of the earliest lessons taught to the aspiring magician was how to shift between two 'levels' of consciousness, from that of ordinary everyday experience (within the physical body) to a higher 'magical' consciousness (within the astral body) that allowed him or her to experience the astral light. Achieving this change was believed necessary to magical success. To this end, adepts employed various processes such as meditation, visualization, and incantation, and on occasion took drugs such as hashish and mescaline. The imagination, it was understood, created an image which could then (as a Golden Dawn document put it) be 'directed and used' by the will. Despite the imagination's role in the process, Golden Dawn members were nonetheless clear that their experiences must not be purely products of their own mind: they were taught to test the beings they encountered carefully, with magical signs and words. (They also needed techniques to protect themselves against anything they met on their travels that should prove unfriendly.)

Mathers made the papers of John Dee a primary resource for understanding magical engagement with the astral light; he constructed a system from the records of the sessions held by

Dee and Edward Kelley, which he termed 'Enochian' magic – the biblical figure Enoch having apparently been a prior recipient of the same angelic language. Mathers himself attempted to use this to call on magical forces, and he made it the basis for a great deal of what went on in the Second Order. He also saw to it that members of this Second Order engaged in divinatory techniques such as geomancy and astrology.

Some magicians saw the astral realms and spirits as symbols for natural forces; as the Theosophist Annie Besant (1847–1933) put it, magic was 'the use of the Will to guide the powers of external nature'. When Annie Horniman and Frederick Leigh Gardner (1857–*c*.1930) met regularly in 1898 in Horniman's

---

CLAIRVOYANCE IN THE GOLDEN DAWN

A Golden Dawn document on clairvoyance instructed initiates to use a symbol (perhaps a drawing or coloured diagram). Touch or hold this image and 'with the utmost concentration, gaze at it, comprehend it, formulate its meaning and relations'. Now, close the eyes and 'let the conception still remain before you'. 'Transfer the Vital effort from the optic nerve to the mental perception', producing by an act of will 'the reality of the dream vision' while awake. Say the highest divine names (this 'produces and harmonises currents of spiritual force in sympathy with your object'), then 'the sacred names of Archangelic and Angelic import, producing them mentally, visually and by voice'. Retaining focus on the symbol, the initiate should 'seek a perception of a scene, panorama, or view of a place'. Success might be accompanied by 'a sense of tearing open' and 'seeing the "within" of the symbol before you'. Finally, 'particularise the details, and seek around for objects, and then for beings, entities, and persons'. Call out mentally to these entities 'by suitable titles and courtesies, and by proper and appropriate signs and symbols'; test them 'by divine and angelic names', observing their responses. They might provide information.

house for astral journeys to visit the planets, they saw themselves as coming to know occult forces and properties associated with those planets. They began the process by making a talisman for each planet they were to visit and focusing on it; they performed a series of rituals each time as preparation and recorded the experiences they had (the places they saw and the beings they met).

The Golden Dawn taught its adepts how to use various symbols as a way of embarking on these astral journeys. Different symbols connected to different (astral) places that the magician could reach through meditation. They included the tarot, and tattvas, derived originally from Hindu philosophies and referring to elements or aspects of reality; in the Golden Dawn, tattvas were represented by simple shapes (a yellow square for earth, a blue circle for air) which could be shown in combination. Each symbol was painted onto a card for use. Stare intently at it, members were told, 'until you seem to see *into* it', or place the card against your forehead 'keeping the eyes closed' – until thoughts of everything else were banished and the magician reached a state of reverie, 'or with a distinctive sense of change, something allied in sensation to a faint, with a feeling urging you to resist, but if you are highly inspired, fear not, do not resist, let yourself go; and then the vision may pass over you'. This done (and a ritual performed), the magician was then to turn the symbol mentally into a doorway to the astral realm and allow his magical consciousness (in its astral, embodied form) to enter it.

There were three basic ways in which magicians drew on the astral light in their work within the Golden Dawn. The first was scrying, using an object or surface such as a mirror (like Dee's, figure 2) to see visions in. A small group in the Golden Dawn attempted this with a clairvoyant medium, following Dee's method, listening to and interpreting the medium's account of those visions. A surviving instruction document explains how to visualize astral realms (actively, not passively like a medium); this was a prelude to the other two (more advanced) ways of engaging with the astral light.

The second was astral travel, sometimes called astral projection: entering the astral realms and interacting with them directly. Magicians had to achieve the sensation of having their 'magical' self embodied separately from their 'mundane' self; that magical body then travelled on the astral planes, able to rise higher the more refined it became. Astral travel was even possible while asleep, according to Golden Dawn members, and they discussed and dissected dreams to reveal the secrets exposed on somnambulistic journeys.

The third main activity was 'rising in the planes', which was linked to the cabbala. Initiates were taught that the cabbala reflected the Hermetic dictum 'As above, so below' taught within the First Order. This was traditionally taken as pointing to a link between man (the 'microcosm') and the universe as a whole (the 'macrocosm'). The Tree of Life was a cabbalistic symbol that represented both the macrocosm and the microcosm, and showed a network of correspondences connecting the two. Figure 5 shows a seventeenth-century representation that was an important source for the Golden Dawn's view of this Jewish mystical representation. The Tree of Life showed connections between 'Sephiroth', divine emanations by means of which the absolute, unchangeable, and unknowable God had created the universe. Each Sephirah was a name for God representing one of his attributes. The Tree of Life showed how all things were interconnected and provided a path towards spiritual enlightenment: 'rising on the planes' involved a practitioner visualizing him or herself moving between the ten Sephiroth.

The Sephiroth had a multitude of associations. First Order initiates learned detailed correspondences between the Sephiroth and, for instance, gemstones, colours, and numbers. The Baphomet image presented by Lévi (figure 4) was pointing upwards to 'the white moon of Chesed' and downwards at 'the

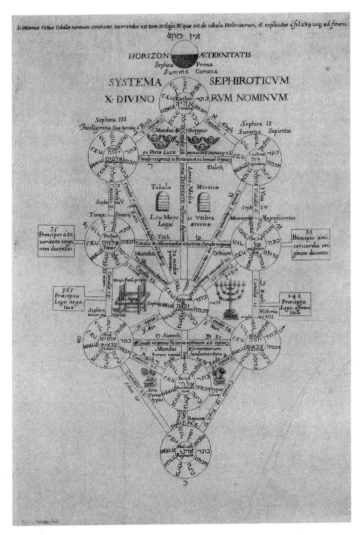

Figure 5 The cabbalistic 'Tree of Life'

black moon of Geburah'. Both of these were Sephiroth: *Chesed* was mercy or grace, *Geburah* justice or judgement. Together, Lévi had written, these formed 'the sign of occultism', 'the perfect concord between mercy and justice'. After Lévi, the twenty-two paths linking the Sephiroth in the Tree were associated with the Hebrew letters and cards of the tarot's major arcana, particular planets, signs of the zodiac, and the four elements, and these too were studied by members of the First Order. Focusing on these in meditation was believed to enable the initiate to achieve a higher level of consciousness, and this was taught in detail in the Second Order. An adept could in theory use techniques based on this knowledge to come to know worlds other than ours and to control invisible forces.

Initiates were instructed that a magical formula correctly intoned could produce a particular change in the magician, some third party, and any world. The magic this made possible was a way of achieving individual perfection – becoming, as they called it, the 'Great' or 'Perfect Man'. The adept could control the universe's hidden forces, could invoke deities and other spiritual entities, and could even take on the characteristics of such a force or the power of such a deity. He or she could communicate with other worlds. In gaining these capacities, the adept was moving towards true enlightenment; at one initiation ceremony, candidates swore that they would apply themselves to 'the Great Work', namely 'to purify and exalt my Spiritual Nature so that with the Divine Aid I may at length attain to be more than human'. The magician would, in a series of meditations, picture him or herself moving up the Tree of Life from the Tenth Sephirah (Malkuth, the Kingdom, constituting the physical world) and encountering the Divine Light as it flowed down from the First Sephirah (Kether, the Crown). By doing this, practitioners sought to achieve mental and spiritual power. At its heart, the Golden Dawn's project was arguably about personal, mental development.

The initiate achieved that development by means of symbols. Symbols, as Yeats explained, could be employed to evoke the 'great mind' and the 'great memory' – concepts he claimed were crucial to understanding magic in the Golden Dawn. The 'great mind' was the coalescence of individual minds, the 'great memory' the 'memory of Nature herself'. Use of the right symbols, verbally and pictorially, allowed the magician to access them. Moreover, the magician's imagination worked with these symbols to engage with what it found in the great mind and the great memory. This was magic as it was correctly understood, he explained; these doctrines had been 'handed down from early times, and been the foundation of nearly all magical practices'. These symbols were drawn from eclectic sources, from the Hindu Tattvas to the tarot arcana that Lévi had made so much of. Kenneth Mackenzie's 1861 discussion with Lévi had concerned the tarot, and Mathers had published on it in 1888; the Golden Dawn was primarily responsible for introducing to the English-speaking world the idea of divination on the basis of tarot cards. In 1910 the Rider–Waite–Smith tarot was published, designed by Golden Dawn members; Waite used Lévi's 'Baphomet' picture as the Devil card.

Symbolism shaped the ritual actions and words used in the Second Order's magic, the tools that practitioners used in the course of their rites, and the clothes they wore while doing it. Advanced initiates made and consecrated their own magical tools, each using a cup, a dagger, a wand, a 'pentacle' (a pentangle engraved on a disc), and a sword; these represented the elements (the cup, water and the wand, fire) or the magician's mental powers. Second Order initiates wore a robe that signified secrecy, and a 'Rose Cross Lantern', a badge that they made and painted to a prescribed (symbolically important) design. Much of the ritual symbolism employed in Golden Dawn rites was alchemical, where 'alchemy' was understood to refer not only to the purification of matter (such as turning base metals into gold) but also to personal development, the perfection of an individual's spirit. Once again, this was magic about developing the self through the proper use of symbols.

Aleister Crowley

One of the century's most famous magicians started out on his magical career as a member of the Golden Dawn. Edward Alexander ('Alick') Crowley had been born in 1875 to a wealthy couple of 'Plymouth Brethren', fundamentalist Christians, and studied at Cambridge from 1895–8. He left with no degree but with an inheritance and strong interests in chess, mountaineering, writing poetry, and occultism. By now he had changed his name to 'Aleister', which he understood to be the Gaelic for 'Alexander'. A chance encounter abroad for a climb led to his introduction to Mathers and his initiation into the Golden Dawn on 18 November 1898 as a Neophyte, under the magical name 'Perdurabo' ('I Will Endure'). He advanced through the hierarchy, reaching the First Order's highest grade in May of the following year, but found the material for study dull; when a respected Second Order magician, Allan Bennett, accused him of meddling with evil forces, Crowley sought his advice and Bennett spent a period living at Crowley's London flat, calling spirits with him and teaching him the magical use of drugs. Crowley was attracting attention, however: senior Golden Dawn members had noted both his homosexuality and his involvement in demonic magic. Yeats thought that he was probably insane. When Crowley was turned down for membership of the Second Order, Mathers supported him from his base in Paris and initiated him into the order there in January 1900. Despite this, as relations within the group became increasingly fraught, Crowley was informed that the London branch were refusing to accept the ceremony's legitimacy. For several days in

April 1900 Crowley occupied the Second Order's rooms in London with written permission from Mathers, before being ejected. As with many Golden Dawn members, Crowley now drifted away and turned to study with other experts.

According to his own account, it was in April 1904 in Cairo that Crowley set down the *Liber AL vel legis* (*The Book of the Law*). His new wife Rose had, as he later reported it, begun to enter involuntary trances and told him that the Egyptian god Horus was waiting to communicate with him; *The Book of the Law* was (he explained) the result, dictated to him over three days by Aiwass, Horus's minister and Crowley's Holy Guardian Angel. Crowley's book was arguably most famous later for a dictum echoed from the work of François Rabelais, the ruling principle of the utopian abbey of Thélème: 'Do what thou wilt shall be the whole of the Law.' As Crowley had it, 'There is no law beyond Do what thou wilt. Love is the law, love under will'. This injunction, ascribed to the Egyptian goddess Nuit, was the 'Law of Thelema'. More broadly, the book (written in a biblical style) announced that the age of Osiris – a resurrected god, presumably signifying Christianity – was to be replaced that year by that of Horus, 'the crowned and conquering child'. Horus was androgynous and this New Aeon could be characterized as unifying male and female; Crowley would be the prophet of this age, the Beast 666. Whatever the details, they were clearly irrelevant to Crowley in 1904; it would be five years before he claimed to have rediscovered the manuscript in his loft and reconsidered its doctrines. In 1904 he was continuing on his travels with his wife and newborn daughter.

His journey ended badly, his daughter dead of typhoid and his wife on a rapid descent into alcoholism. By 1906 he was experimenting with drugs once more, and returning to earlier interests in the ceremonial and cabbalistic magic disclosed in an old magic text translated by Mathers as *The Sacred Magic of Abramerlin the Mage* (1897). He now began to construct his own magical order, Astrum Argenteum (Silver Star), and launched a periodical to accompany it: *The Equinox*, devoted to serious occultist discussion. By 1907 he was looking for people to join his new order. Captain John Frederick Charles Fuller of the British Army was an early recruit who co-edited *The Equinox*. Fuller in turn introduced Crowley to a poet studying at Cambridge, Victor Neuburg; Crowley gave Neuburg a long reading list and set out to teach him self-discipline through physical exertion, taking him on a walk across the Pyrenees and down through Spain to Gibraltar. After finishing his degree in June 1909, Neuburg joined Crowley at his house by Loch Ness to find that his next task was a Magical Retirement, which (it turned out) meant ten days of withdrawal to a special room to find and explore the astral light while enduring physical hardships and eating little. Slow progress was rewarded with scourging and Neuburg was subjected to continual, often racist, insults. Neuburg began with basic knowledge taught by Crowley: protective rites and procedures; the importance of keeping particular tools and implements (including a ritual sword) close at hand. Incense would help create the right atmosphere. Finally, on the third day, Neuburg achieved what he and Crowley recognized as success: yoga and meditation eventually brought him the experience of astral travel. Over the next few days, Neuburg found achieving these states increasingly easy, and noted down detailed accounts of his journeys, describing meetings with giants and warriors and visits to the courts of Egyptian gods. Meanwhile, according to Crowley, the manuscript *Book of the Law* had resurfaced in the loft; after meditating on it, he said, he had finally accepted its message and his mission as the establishment of the Law it contained. By the autumn Crowley was itching to leave the country to avoid being present for his divorce, which had reached court. Crowley and Neuburg arrived at Algiers in North Africa on 17 November.

They headed immediately for the desert in the south west, Neuburg now shaven-headed with two tufts of hair sculpted into horns. They walked for several days, sleeping in the open. Crowley had brought magical materials with him and he decided to resume earlier experiments in the so-called 'Enochian' magic systematized by Mathers from John Dee's records, with its thirty Aethyrs or Aires, distinct destinations for astral travel. Members of the Golden Dawn's Second Order studied the system; Crowley, who was familiar with it, wanted to carry out its practical procedures. He had copied out Dee's nineteen Calls or Keys, excerpts in the angelic language used, among other things, to invoke these 'Aethyrs'; he now used the Calls to go on astral journeys. Crowley played Kelley's part in the proceedings, using a large topaz to look into and describing visions to Neuburg for transcription. He reported talking to celestial beings and later described slowly coming to trust the experiences while becoming conscious of a growing dread, against which he recited the Qur'an as he walked.

Two weeks in, Crowley prepared a magical rite in honour of the god Pan at Bou Saada, an oasis town in the desert. He had (he said) been instructed to do this, but also warned that he was going into 'the Kingdom of the Grave'. He arranged a circle with rocks, inscribed with words of power, and built an altar within it; the ceremony centred on sex between Neuburg and Crowley. In the aftermath of the ritual Crowley decided that he must now attempt to 'cross the Abyss' – a last, terrifying act to be performed by anyone in his Silver Star order trying to become a Master of the Temple. He was to attempt this in the tenth Aethyr and expected to face a powerful devil called Choronzon, who would overcome him and enslave him if he failed, bringing disaster and failure forever after. In a desert valley on 6 December they traced a circle and a triangle in the sand and wrote 'Choronzon' by the triangle and divine names round both. The circle would protect them and the triangle would contain the demon. They sacrificed three pigeons and anointed the triangle's corners with the blood. Crowley entered the triangle while Neuburg stayed in the circle; Neuburg afterwards described Choronzon appearing in successive forms (an attractive woman, a holy man, a serpent), and eventually breaking the circle and entering to fight him before Neuburg could drive him back to the triangle. On Choronzon's disappearance Crowley had signalled to him that he had defeated the demon. Crowley, for his part, explained that he had identified with Choronzon throughout, experiencing the demon's emotions. Two hours after the ceremony's start it ended with a fire to purify the site. Though the two men carried out further rituals over the following days they were exhausted, and sailed for England on 31 December.

By now Crowley had used up his inheritance and was finding it increasingly difficult to make ends meet. He and Neuburg continued to experiment with combining sex and magic, till in 1914 Neuburg told Crowley that he wanted to stop. Crowley pronounced a ritual curse on him and Neuburg suffered a breakdown.

In 1912 Crowley was initiated into the Ordo Templi Orientis in Germany, a relatively young order whose leader (frater superior) Theodor Reuss had sought him out. The group had been established in 1904, another offshoot of Freemasonry, influenced partly by Lévi's writings and the familiar myth of the hidden wisdom of the Knights Templar (whose descent the group claimed), and partly by Indian traditions, yoga and tantra. Its focus was on sex magic, which it held was at the root of the symbolism used by Hermetic writers and Freemasons. The order's highest grades involved autoerotic and heterosexual magic, and intercourse was treated as the holiest of all religious sacraments. Crowley impressed Reuss enough to become head of the British and Irish branch of the order, taking the name 'Baphomet'; he altered some of the rituals and introduced a high grade relating to homosexual magic, combining the order's practices with parts of his *Book of the Law.*

Crowley now believed that magical rites and invocations were most successful when combined with particular sex acts, and he continued to experiment with sex magic, recording his activities with various sexual partners in diaries after his move to America where he produced German propaganda during the First World War. He had also adopted the spelling 'magick', the added 'k' bearing various symbolic meanings and the new word clearly distinguishing ritual practice from stage illusion. At its most basic, 'magick' for Crowley was an all-embracing term that encompassed such mundane actions as writing on paper alongside more exotic rituals. Magick was, he explained, 'the Science and Art of causing Change to occur in conformity with Will'; magical ritual was specifically about harnessing the universe's powers for the individual by 'the uniting of the Microcosm with the Macrocosm'. The Will to which these actions conformed was specifically True Will rather than conscious will – in other words, it was a person's inner nature, to be ignored at his or her peril. More specifically, Crowley's 'magick' included much that was similar to the Golden Dawn's teachings (rituals and the means of preparing for them, astral travel), as well as procedures centred on sexual acts.

In 1920 Crowley established himself in Cefalù, in Sicily. He rented a farmhouse there with Leah Hirsig and called it the Abbey of Thelema, writing the legend 'Do What Thou Wilt' over the doorway and calling himself 'the Beast 666'. Many of the men and women who went to join him there returned home with shocking stories. Crowley's rituals reportedly involved pain and bodily fluids and centred on sexual acts. Crowley enlarged on his fundamental Law by explaining that everyone 'has an absolute right to satisfy his sexual instinct as is physiologically proper for him'. The only injunction, he added, 'is to treat all such acts as sacraments'. Eventually stories of the orgies taking place there spread to the press, and the periodical *John Bull* ran a story labelling Crowley 'the wickedest man in the world'. Crowley, meanwhile, was taking over Reuss's role as head of the Ordo Templi Orientis (around the time of Reuss's death). Finally, in 1923, a disciple from London died at the Sicilian farmhouse and, although the death was put down to natural causes, Mussolini's government expelled the group from Italy.

Life was now increasingly difficult for Crowley, having long since run through his inheritance and having attracted the opprobrium of the popular press; he attempted litigation but with little success. He continued to write and remained a focus of interest for occultists, who corresponded with and visited him. Nonetheless, he died in Hastings on 1 December 1947, aged seventy-two, penurious and heroin-addicted. Through his writings and his encounters he influenced the majority of the occult and pagan groups in existence since then.

Modern pagan witchcraft

Occultism in early twentieth-century Europe was closely allied to a resurgence of paganism. This in turn linked it to the rise of fascist parties across the continent. An Italian polymath and right-wing philosopher called Julius Evola (1898–1974) had been studying magical and alchemical texts for several years when in 1927 he co-founded the Gruppo di Ur, an organization whose purpose was to foster a return to the pagan religion of Roman antiquity in support of Italian fascism. In 1930s Germany, Karl Maria Wiligut (1866–1946) constructed the apparatus of an official pagan religion for the Nazi regime. These were connections that would tarnish paganism in Europe for years after the end of the Second World War. There are examples of other early pagan groups without such alarming associations – the Church of Aphrodite, for instance, established on Long Island in the United States in 1938. Nonetheless, based on what we know of these organizations, they seem to have been rather small-scale affairs.

That paganism has become a worldwide fascination in the decades since then is chiefly the result of the activities of one Englishman. Gerald Brosseau Gardner (1884–1964), having retired to the New Forest in England in the 1930s, described encountering a witch coven and being initiated into their religion. This religion, Gardner claimed, was a modern survival of pre-Christian paganism; he identified the coven's activities with the ancient tradition reported by the folklorist Margaret Murray (1863–1963), who argued that the witches persecuted by Christian authorities for centuries had been pagans worshipping a horned god. In 1946, Gardner wrote a novel (published in 1949) in which he incorporated what he later claimed to be details of the witches' practices. In the same year he was also involved in buying and relocating a modern impression of a sixteenth-century, half-timbered witch's cottage decorated inside with cabbalistic symbols, which became a centre for the coven's activities. By December he was on the governing council of the Circle of the Universal Bond (the Ancient Druid Order).

Gardner approached Aleister Crowley and spent four days with him in May 1947, not long before Crowley's death. Contemporary documents suggest that Gardner was keen on reviving the Ordo Templi Orientis in England, where it had lapsed with the onset of war and Crowley's diminishing health; they also reveal that he himself had reached the seventh grade within the order. Gardner reported at this stage that Crowley had been very interested in his coven, and for many years afterwards (according to one associate) Gardner talked 'reverently' of him. Certainly influences are detectable in rituals and invocations. However, by the time Gardner reported the meeting to his biographer, over a decade later, it had become clear that he needed some distance from Crowley and all that was associated with him in the public imagination. Hence the 1960 account (which misdated the encounter to 1946) explained that Gardner had been initiated into the OTO but had seen Crowley as 'a charming charlatan'. Whatever the case, by the time of Crowley's death at the end of 1947, Gardner was more focused on pagan witchcraft than on the OTO.

Over the course of several years at the end of the 1940s, Gardner compiled texts and rituals into two notebooks: first, 'Ye Bok of ye Art Magical', and later, the 'Book of Shadows'. The earlier of these contained biblical verses and copies of older magical texts (referred to in the modern period as 'grimoires'), as well as material on cabbala, books by Crowley, and the

GARDNER RECOUNTS A PAGAN WITCH'S SPELL

Among the rituals recorded by Gardner in the *Book of Shadows* was a spell he regarded as particularly effective. The subject, bound tightly at the wrists, knees, and feet to restrict the blood, was to be scourged '40 or more, to make the skin tingle', and would then say ('invoking the Goddess'): 'Hail, Aradia, from the Amalthean horn Pour forth thy store of Love. I lowly bend Before Thee! I invoke thee at the end When other Gods are fallen and put to scorn. Thy foot is to my lips! My sighs inborn Rise, touch, curl about thy heart. Then spend, Pitiful Love, loveliest Pity, descend And bring me luck who am lonely and forlorn.' Gardner continued: 'Ask the Goddess to help you to obtain your desires, then Scourge again to bind the spell.' This procedure was 'powerful in ill luck and for sickness', and was to be performed in a ritual circle by two people who would prepare and undergo purification both beforehand and afterwards, 'to bind the spell'. 'Make yourself see the wish obtained', he instructed. 'Be sure in your own mind exactly what it is and how it is to be fulfilled.'

Rider–Waite–Smith tarot pack. The later volume constituted nothing less than a set of instructions and a sacred text for the religion.

The body, in the witchcraft religion, was to be considered sacred, and power was available to those who treated it in particular ways – through nudity in rituals (to allow free release of the body's natural powers) and the judicious use of binding and scourging to aid entry into ecstatic trances. Sex was a central element as was the drawing down of spiritual entities (gods and goddesses) into the people involved in the rites. Participants used tools: a sword, two daggers (one black-handled, one white-handled), a wand, a censer, a pentacle (in this case a disc engraved with a pentagram), a cord and a scourge. The black-handled knife ('athame') was to be used to make magic circles and to control conjured spirits.

Debts to predecessors, such as Crowley, Lévi, and the Golden Dawn, were clear, both in the details of the rites and in the overall structure: there were grades of ritual participation and a hierarchy, derived (at least in the lower levels) from Freemasonry and requiring instruction to move through. Rituals, which marked the four seasons and included fertility dances and the consumption of consecrated food and drink, would be led by a high priestess and a high priest, and performed in reverence of a goddess and a horned god. The goddess was predominant in winter, the god in summer. In its detailed description of ritual practices, the 'Book of Shadows' provided a schema for the religion when Gardner went public in the 1950s; nonetheless, he himself only published extracts from it. Others had copies printed after his death in 1964, and a critical edition was produced in the 1980s.

By 1950, Gardner had embarked on a campaign to spread word of the witchcraft religion. He was already telling members of London's networks of occult practitioners; after the Witchcraft and Vagrancy Acts were repealed in 1951, making witchcraft no longer a prosecutable offence, he turned to the national press. He was also working on a book that would allow him to explain the religion at length. *Witchcraft Today* was published in 1954. In it, Gardner portrayed himself as an anthropologist revealing that witchcraft had secretly survived. He also gave the religion a name: he called it 'Wica' (probably from the *Chambers* Scots dictionary, where the word was defined as 'wise'), and explained that 'Wica' meant 'wise people'. In the following years it became 'Wicca', in line with an Anglo-Saxon term for a male witch. Despite the pose struck by Gardner in *Witchcraft Today*, academic reviewers (then and now) have tended to treat his claims of discovery with disbelief. Members of the Folk-Lore Society responding to his book contrasted his picture of witchcraft unfavourably with the traditional attitudes they themselves had uncovered. These details did not deter everyone, however, and his campaign certainly worked to attract newcomers.

In some cases Gardner's attempts to create publicity backfired spectacularly; from 1951 the press began to run stories about his group practising devil-worship, with a renewal of the attack in 1955–6. The coven diverged over whether the best response was retreat and focus on books (where there was at least certainty of editorial control), or whether the newspapers remained the best option, presuming that potential members would be able to see beyond the negative portrayals. The mounting row, and a suspicion that Gardner was running things on a rather more ad hoc basis than his continual references to ancient tradition indicated, led to a split in 1957; eventually, in January 1959, after *The People* had revealed the identities of people involved in the coven, the group dispersed. Gardner continued to initiate more or less anyone who approached him, with the result that in the late 1950s and early 1960s a number of high priestesses emerged who would go on to establish covens across England and Scotland – and, in 1963, the United States.

Gardner defended Wicca from its detractors in his last book, published in 1959, then established a canonical account of his discovery of pagan witchcraft for a biography written in 1960. He died in 1964.

Gardner's tradition began to attract attention in the United States through the 1960s. Moreover, witchcraft, its history and practice, became associated with feminist politics in the 1970s. Witchcraft was female power, subversive of male dominance – an interpretation applied by many to the witch trials. This was a period in which another (superficially similar) movement took an interest in paganism and witchcraft: New Age. It is an association that persists in popular culture, despite all attempts by pagans to shake it off. By the 1970s, the United States was paganism's new home. In San Francisco in 1979, Miriam Simos (b. 1951), writing as 'Starhawk', produced one of the most influential books on pagan witchcraft – one whose popularity eclipsed even that of Gardner's *Witchcraft Today*. *The Spiral Dance* provided a new account of witchcraft and its potential as a force for personal and social good. She worked to show how the practices and attitudes encouraged within pagan covens could further a feminist agenda and alter the ways in which men and women related, for the better. At the heart of her project was her understanding of magic as a tool for self-discovery and personal development, or, as she put it, 'part of the discipline of developing "power-from-within"'. It was a means to open 'the gates between the unconscious and the conscious mind'. Spells, she wrote, 'allow us not only to listen to and interpret the unconscious but also to speak to it, in the language it understands'. In the years since this book, Wicca has become increasingly visible internationally. In Europe the Pan-European Wiccan Convention was started in 1990.

Whatever the status of Gardner's witchcraft religion, his was not the only approach in mid-twentieth-century England. Participants in rituals of the 1960s 'Clan of Tubal Cain', founded by Robert Cochrane (1931–66), wore black robes, eschewed the scourge, and used slightly different tools from their Gardnerian counterparts (one knife, a cup, a stone, a forked staff or 'stang'). Males led worship rather than females, and the rites took place around fires. Around the same time Alex Sanders (1926–88) was establishing what became known as 'Alexandrian' Wicca; here, ceremonial magic of the kind practised by members of the Golden Dawn was included as rituals. In the United States, Wicca flourished and divided, with the list of traditions growing through the 1970s and since. 'Dianic' Wicca (for instance) is a feminist form, practised largely in women-only covens and in veneration specifically of the goddess; 'Blue Star' Wicca, represented by a seven-pointed star (septegram) rather than a five-pointed one (pentagram), is distinguished by the use of music in rituals. The examples could be multiplied.

Modern occultism has centred on such groups since the 'occult revival', and it has concerned at its heart occultism as religion. From the Golden Dawn to Wicca, it has championed magical rituals and texts as being part of a tradition that transcends and predates Christianity (or other larger scale religions). Occultists have tended to be syncretists, blending elements and doctrines of Eastern and Western philosophies and religions. They have seen the magic they have espoused as a way of engaging with phenomena and realms beyond the reach of modern science – a way of achieving a different consciousness and effecting changes in themselves and the world at large by means of ritual and meditation.

However, while occultists have understood magic as a secret tradition promising wisdom beyond the rational, others came to see it as a stage *on the way* to becoming rational. The equation was simple: Europeans in past ages had practised magic; non-Europeans in the present day seemed to believe in something similar. Anthropologists reasoned that magical beliefs must be a

point in a society's development – somewhere along a continuum that included religion and ended with science. Travellers,
and particularly missionaries, had long used the word 'magic' to
describe the mysterious practices of the native peoples they
encountered. Now the developing field of anthropology built
these reports into theories of the nature of magic. This is the
topic of the last chapter.

5

Analysing magic

In 1878, John Nevil Maskelyne published an account of how Indian fakirs achieved their feats. He rejected suggestions (often by spiritualists) that these deeds – particularly the fabled Indian rope trick – were evidence of actual magical ability. The East, he explained, was the home of magic – 'not the innocent conjuring we give that name to in England ... but the crafty and sometimes audacious imposture in which the magician pretends to possess supernatural powers, and so beguiles the simple people.' He was referring not so much to China and Japan, which seemed to him 'to have been free from any taint of this kind', though they excelled in accomplishments requiring 'nice mechanism and long practice' such as plate-spinning and knife-throwing. His attention instead was drawn to India, 'one of the cradles of magic and divination', which 'retains trickery as part of its religion to this day'. Indian fakirs, he continued, had 'deluded innocent Englishmen into writing of their jugglery as though it had an element of the miraculous in it.'

Through many years of colonialist expansion by European powers, magic (a term which had originated essentially as racist abuse) became associated with the non-Western societies that they subjugated. When anthropology emerged as a discipline early in the twentieth century, chiefly concerned with understanding the beliefs and practices of the 'savages' who populated these lands, some of its key writers produced works discussing magic. This final chapter examines that tradition of writing, and the role that magic came to play in understandings of alien cultures – and, in turn, the role that those cultures came to play in our understanding of magic.

Non-Western magic

In a strong sense, of course, magic had been treated as mysterious and foreign from the word's first use. When the Greeks and Romans described someone's activities as 'magic' they had in mind the suspicious (and most definitely un-Greek or un-Roman) activities of the magi. The alienness of the rituals ascribed to these men was one of the term's most direct associations. Through the Middle Ages, similar feelings persisted. It was a familiar step, for instance, to turn the unchristian practices of Jews into 'magical incantations', the reason given by the chronicler Matthew Paris for their exclusion from the coronation of Richard I in 1189.

Perhaps most renowned for its magical associations was Egypt. A number of medieval criticisms of magic referred to the attempts by Pharaoh's 'wise men and sorcerers' to match the miracles performed by Moses. Hermes Trismegistus, known through the Middle Ages from a brief text called the 'Emerald Tablet' and the supposed author of a body of texts translated into Latin by Marsilio Ficino, was understood to have been an Egyptian sage; the most learned magic that flourished in the Renaissance was therefore believed to derive from Egypt, even if its provenance was ultimately divine (or at least, divinely sanctioned). So central was magic believed to have been to the Egyptian understanding of the world that both Agrippa and Della Porta recited that 'the *Ægyptians* termed Nature her self a Magician' who brought things together by an affinity that they called 'love'. The perceived association of Egypt with magic extended to Gypsies, who were believed to hail from the same place. Samuel Rid, in a book of 1612, was clear that they had brought to England much of the street juggling around him:

> Certaine Egiptians banished their cuntry … ariued heere in England, who being excellent in quaint trickes and deuises, not known heere at that time among vs, were esteemed and had in

great admiration, for what with strangenesse of their attire and garments, together with their sleights and legerdemaines, they were spoke of farre and neere, insomuch that many of our English loyterers ioyned with them, and in time learned their craft and cosening.

The nineteenth century was a fruitful period in Egyptology, and the field's developments and discoveries were taken up enthusiastically by modern occultists such as the founders of the Golden Dawn. These practitioners looked back to Egypt just as their predecessors had, but now they had further information to support and flesh out their interests. A collection of spells from Greco-Roman Egypt, for instance, came to light early in the century and has provided considerable information about Egyptian practices, the ways in which words were used to invoke gods and effect change. Inspired by such scholarship (and perhaps by the growing craze for all things Egyptian), occultists included Egyptian motifs and gods in their rituals; they proudly linked the cabbala back to Egypt via Moses' sojourn there; and they emphasized their debt to Christian Rosencreutz, who was understood to have visited Egypt – one of the early lessons learned by initiates was that Rosicrucians owed much of their magic to the ancient Egyptians. The Golden Dawn's cipher manuscript referred to ancient Egyptian texts, and its designation as 'Hermetic' similarly pointed to this inheritance.

Such imputations were not limited to the old world. To colonists arriving in North America in the sixteenth and seventeenth centuries, the natives were clearly the children of the devil, utterly unaware of God; according to one Cambridge theologian they had been led by the devil to the New World from Europe. So when those colonists encountered the 'pawwaws', members of native tribes who dealt with the spirit world, particularly to help people who fell ill or to stave off misfortune, they described them as witches, sorcerers, conjurors.

Pawwaws provided herbs and charms, pulled faces, made noises, and beat their chests to draw off spirits apparently responsible for particular diseases. They worked hard to propitiate an evil spirit to prevent it from causing harm. Christians identified this evil spirit as the devil and the pawwaws as devil-worshippers. They blamed these men for difficulties faced by all kinds of expeditions from those of sixteenth-century explorers such as Francis Drake to the military ventures of New England armies in 1637 and 1675. Likewise, Massachusetts frontiersmen encountered 'strange Disasters' because pawwaws had 'Enchanted the Ground'. The mediatory and protective actions of pawwaws were transformed into magic by the invaders, partly because of the resemblance of the practices to more familiar European magic, and partly because of the theological and philosophical framework within which the newcomers viewed the natives.

Explorers were also taking their prejudices to Africa; in the eighteenth century the French engraver and author Bernard Picart wrote of the Khoikhoi ('Hottentots') that:

> These barbarous illiterate People are of Opinion, like the rest of their Neighbours, that the Living are daily exposed to the Misfortune of being charmed, and the Dead of being raised by magical Incantations. Every Transaction which surpasses their weak Comprehensions, is look'd upon by them as the Result of Sorcery and Fascination: The most regular Effects of Nature they ascribe to the irresistible Force of Magick, and can by no Arguments, how cogent soever, be prevail'd on to swerve from their establish'd Notions on any new Emergency.

This association of magic with other cultures was explored most comprehensively in the nineteenth century, as the colonialist project flourished. The beliefs and practices of native peoples were recorded and categorized as 'primitive' and 'magical': reports of this kind provided an intellectual justification for

AN EIGHTEENTH-CENTURY ACCOUNT OF AN AFRICAN HEALING RITUAL

Bernard Picart, cataloguing religious customs, described an African rite for curing an illness:

> The *Cafres* ascribe all their Distempers to the Spells, or Charms of their Enemies, and by consequence, such Physicians as they apply themselves to for Relief, must be Adepts, as it were, in Magic ... Their first Operation ... is the Sacrifice of a fat Weather [a sheep]; after that, the Doctor very gravely examines the *Omentum* [part of the entrails] of the Victim, strews the Powder of *Buchu* [a herb] very plentifully over it; and then hangs it reeking-hot about the Neck of his Patient, with this formal Declaration; *You are enchanted, 'tis true, but I'll engage you shall be well again in a short Time; for the Charm you lie under is but weak, and will easily be dissolved.* The Patient is order'd to wear this Collar, till it rots off his Neck; but if this Prescription proves ineffectual, the Physician enters on a new Scheme, exerts all the Skill he is Master of another way, and has recourse to the secret Virtue of a Variety of Simples, or medicinal Herbs, which he collects in some remote and unfrequented Places.

replacing the existing local institutions of government with something considered more enlightened, rational, and Western.

During the nineteenth century (as Maskelyne's example shows) it became important for Western conjurors to explain away the alleged deeds of Indian wonder-workers as they had the phenomena of spiritualist séances. At the century's beginning it was not uncommon to find Indian and Chinese jugglers in Western countries; the fascination with exotic tricks and illusions of distant origin persisted, but from the 1830s non-white magic lost popularity, and audiences saw the same tricks performed by Western magicians – and sometimes Western magicians imitating (for instance) Chinese or Indian magicians. Through the great period of stage magic its performers, while making use of Eastern stereotypes, were principally white. While Western magicians were genteel, respectable, and intellectually unimpeachable, their Eastern counterparts remained victims of cultural associations that had otherwise been abandoned: credulity, fraud, devilry. Too much was at stake in the imperialist project, with its accounts of credulous natives, to accept that 'Enlightened' magic might be the province of other races. That credulity, where it was positively identified, could prove useful for colonial authorities. In 1856 Napoleon III's government asked the fifty-one-year-old illusionist Jean-Eugène Robert-Houdin to visit Algeria, where French authorities were concerned at unrest fomented by locals who claimed magical powers; Robert-Houdin went to demonstrate that his abilities (and by extension those of the French more generally) were superior. He reported performing several impressive tricks, including catching bullets between his teeth, and rendering a volunteer unable to lift a small box (ostensibly by magically removing his strength; in fact, by fixing the box to the stage using an electromagnet). The mission was apparently successful.

Ultimately, the ad hoc use of the word 'magic' by travellers to describe the beliefs and activities of those they encountered led to a more systematic deployment. In the later years of the nineteenth century, led by such luminaries as Edward Tylor and James Frazer, anthropology was established as an academic field. Informed by the reports of government officials, travellers, and missionaries, Tylor and Frazer worked to establish universal theories of the development of mankind; looking at accounts from across the world and throughout history, they sought to understand religion, magic, and science and the relationships between them. It is to the anthropological debates on magic, fed directly from these travellers' reports, that I now turn.

Reason and disenchantment

The idea that magic was a step on the way to science is still with us, in intricate academic debates and in throwaway remarks. We owe the notion to the grand theories of Sir Edward Burnett Tylor (1832–1917) and Sir James Frazer (1854–1941), who fitted magic into their evolutionary schemes of how mankind developed from 'savagery' to that epitome of civilization, the modern West. The scale of the vision offered by Tylor and Frazer was chiefly down to their distance from their subjects; they were too far away from the societies they were writing about, and too reliant on others' descriptions of them, to engage with the finer details. As Frazer put it, it was precisely the fact that he treated the library as his territory and did not explore the world that permitted him to achieve his bird's-eye view without succumbing to the fascination of specific details. A classicist by training, he combined present-day eyewitness records with ancient texts. He spent most of his working life at his desk in Trinity College, Cambridge, analysing the reports of explorers, missionaries, and government officials and cataloguing the beliefs and practices they documented. Likewise, although Tylor's interest in anthropology was first piqued on a four-month expedition to Mexico, the primary basis for his theorizing was travellers' accounts. Only this kind of study would allow researchers to identify 'universal' human concepts, beliefs, and practices – such as magic.

Tylor focused principally on concepts and beliefs. In his 1871 book *Primitive culture* he recounted the development of culture in general and religion in particular. Culture he defined as 'knowledge, belief, art, morals, law, custom, and any other capabilities and habits acquired by man as a member of society'; religion he understood to be 'the belief in Spiritual Beings'. Belief, in other words, was primary – and so was the individual. Societies do not believe things or think things, people do: at the heart of Tylor's theory was the individual and the individual's thoughts. Thus, in his account the earliest form of religion ('animism') came about by a process of reasoning: 'primitive' people came to believe that souls provided the difference between the living and the dead, and gave rise to the appearance in dreams and visions of things that looked human; they then generalized from people to things, taking it that animals and even objects such as stones have souls too. This animist world would seem to be governed by souls and spirits rather than by any law or mechanical principle. In time, animism would give way to polytheism (the belief in many gods), then to monotheism. Each shift in religion would be driven by a rational process – a thought that gave rise to a belief.

Tylor saw belief in magic as a straightforward and understandable (if mistaken) stage in humanity's development. He included divinatory practices such as astrology under its rubric. Magic had coexisted with animism in primitive societies, and it arose from a confusion of ideas. The eighteenth-century philosopher David Hume had noted that people mentally linked things where they resembled each other (a portrait and its subject), where they were next to one other (different apartments in the same building), and when one caused another (a wound and pain). In 'primitive' societies, Tylor explained, people simply confused the first two forms of association with the last one: they mistook associations of resemblance and contiguity with causal links. The cockerel always crows when the sun rises, the thought goes, so forcing the cockerel to crow will make the sun rise. Such associations could be powerful and tricky to refute – when the sun eventually rose the magic would appear to be successful, even if the effect was not immediate. Delayed successful outcomes were still successful outcomes.

Frazer put it more clearly (and at greater length): magic was a failed attempt at science. For Frazer, magic was 'a spurious system of natural law as well as a fallacious guide of conduct; it is a false science as well as an abortive art'. It was a set of mistaken ideas (a 'false science'), but first and foremost it was an ineffective practice (an 'abortive art'). It divided into 'positive magic', or sorcery (do X so that Y happens) and 'negative magic' or taboo (do not do X, or Y will happen). Where Tylor had written of principles of association as key to understanding magic, Frazer divided these into two types, two broad principles on which magic was based.

The first was the 'Law of Similarity': like produces like, so that an effect resembles its cause. This principle produced 'Homeopathic or Imitative Magic'. A magician practising this believed that he could produce an effect simply by imitating it. Frazer explained, in a sentence that reveals the extent of his explanatory ambitions, that it was a principle that could be found

FRAZER AND THE ANCIENT HINDU JAUNDICE CURE

Frazer recounted as an example of 'homeopathic magic' a ceremony performed by 'ancient Hindoos' to cure jaundice by returning the unhealthy colour to naturally yellow things and replacing it with healthy red from a bull. The patient drank water mixed with bull's hair and some run off its back, sat on bull skin and was tied to a piece of it; then smeared with a turmeric paste, laid on a bed to which a parrot, a thrush, and a yellow wagtail were tethered, and the turmeric washed off again. As he worked, the priest would say: 'Up to the sun shall go thy heart-ache and thy jaundice: in the colour of the red bull do we envelop thee! We envelop thee in red tints, unto long life. May this person go unscathed and be free of yellow colour! The cows whose divinity is Rohini, they who, moreover, are themselves red (*rohinih*) – in their every form and every strength we do envelop thee. Into the parrots, into the thrush, do we put thy jaundice, and, furthermore, into the yellow wagtail do we put thy jaundice.' Finally, more red bull hairs were wrapped in gold leaf and glued to the patient's skin.

across the world and throughout history: 'thousands of years ago it was known to the sorcerers of ancient India, Babylon, and Egypt, as well as of Greece and Rome', he wrote, 'and at this day it is still resorted to by cunning and malignant savages in Australia, Africa, and Scotland.' His examples added America and Asia to the list: 'an Ojebway Indian' who wanted to harm someone, he reported, 'makes a little wooden image of his enemy and runs a needle into its head or heart'; similarly, 'among the Bataks of Sumatra', a woman who wanted to become a mother would 'make a wooden image of a child and hold it in her lap'.

The second principle of magic was the 'Law of Contact or Contagion': things that had once been in contact with each other would continue to act on one another even after physically separated. It too had worldwide applicability and was illustrated with countless examples. Frazer discussed at length examples from Australian tribes where boys undergoing rituals to be accepted as men had front teeth knocked out; there was, he explained, a belief 'that a sympathetic relation continued to exist between the lad and his teeth after the latter had been extracted from his gums', so that the teeth were to be looked after lest their former owner be harmed.

In practice, contagious magic usually also involved applying the principle of 'Homeopathic Magic', and the two were probably seldom separated. Together they were 'Sympathetic Magic', both assuming action at a distance through some kind of 'secret sympathy'. Archetypal magic, for Frazer, consisted of such operations as the Malay charm which involved making a likeness of some person with a mixture of wax and some substances derived from that person (nail parings, saliva, hair), then holding the figure over a lamp every night for seven nights to scorch it, saying:

It is not wax that I am scorching,
It is the liver, heart, and spleen of So-and-so that I scorch.

The figure was to be burned on the final occasion, killing the victim. The logic behind sympathetic magic was also observed in reverse: taboos, he argued, were about magic just as the manipulation of images was. (Others have since disagreed.) He outlined the foods that soldiers in Madagascar were expected to avoid: they should not eat hedgehog because it might communicate its timidity to them, or ox's knee lest they become similarly weak at the knees; moreover, no male animal could be killed at a soldier's house when he was away fighting, or he might himself be killed in the same way and possibly at the same time.

So magic was based on flawed principles; but it was false *science* because it shared important characteristics with science. 'Wherever sympathetic magic occurs in its pure unadulterated form', Frazer wrote, 'it assumes that in nature one event follows another necessarily and invariably without the intervention of any spiritual or personal agency.' This fundamental assumption (or 'faith', as he called it) was shared by magic and science: the 'order and uniformity of nature'. The same causes would always produce the same effects; performing a ceremony correctly in all its details would achieve the desired result (unless countered by the actions of a more powerful person). Magic was 'the bastard sister of science', by definition 'false and barren'; were it to become true and fruitful it would be science. That body of maxims accumulated by societies over time could by divided simply into the 'true or golden rules', which 'constitute the body of applied science which we call the arts', and 'the false' – which were magic.

This focus on the falsity of magic created a problem: did this mean that its practitioners were deceivers? Tylor's response was that they sometimes were but not necessarily: magic may be false, but it isn't necessarily fraudulent. If a practitioner was fraudulent, he could use a combination of legerdemain and rhetorical skill to convince an audience of his veracity; on the other hand, it was possible for such a person to be taken in by his own art. His predictions might be vague; he might be able to ascribe his failures to breaching important conditions, or interference from some other party; he might simply not appreciate evidence for his magic's ineffectiveness. Ultimately, Tylor believed, people persevered in practising the false, superstitious magical arts out of conservatism rather than outright fraud; it proved difficult to abandon such long-held notions. That difficulty was precisely why an anthropological analysis of magic was useful, to help people break away from their bad habits.

If Tylor saw the glass as half-full, for Frazer it was half-empty. He admitted that while sorcerers often believed quite sincerely that they possessed the powers ascribed to them, the wiser practitioners must surely see through magic's 'fallacies', so that the ablest magicians, he wrote, 'tend to be more or less conscious deceivers'. As a result, those who achieved power tended to be the cleverest and most unscrupulous. Tribes believed that their welfare depended on magicians, so magicians tended to rise to influence – they might even, he carried on, 'readily acquire the rank and authority of a chief or king'. The combination of intelligence, ambition, and deceit was a dangerous one.

Frazer's account has been the most enduring, and perhaps this is partly down to its simplicity: in his evolutionary scheme, societies moved chronologically from magic, to religion, to science. Frazer agreed with Tylor that magic's falsity (and ineffectiveness) was 'far from easy to detect', as many of the events that magic was supposed to bring about happened anyway: the rising of the sun, the arrival of rain. Even the death of an enemy would come eventually. Nonetheless, Frazer was confident that at some point 'the more thoughtful part of mankind' would begin to recognize the 'falsehood and barrenness of magic', seeing at last that the ceremonies and incantations had no effect and that the world carried on without aid. The 'primitive philosopher' would then reason that if the world continued in its course without human ceremonies, that must be because there was a more powerful being directing it instead. That being should therefore be the object of pleading and propitiation. This would be the beginning of religion. (All of this, Frazer explained, would take 'long ages'.)

The influential German sociologist Max Weber (1864–1920) charted the erosion of magic via a process he called the 'disenchantment of the world'. Disenchantment was most evident in the West: the developments of Protestantism, the Enlightenment, and even capitalism were all aspects of this broader change. Puritans provided a particularly clear example: a true Puritan, Weber wrote, eschewed religious ceremony even during burials, 'in order that no superstition, no trust in the effects of magical and sacramental forces on salvation, should creep in'. The ideas and practices ruled out were those that gave meaning to the smallest aspects of daily life; in the disenchanted world, people sought meaning in rationality, relying on intellect. The end-point of rationalization would be a world whose inhabitants believed it possible to 'master all things by calculation'. The archetypal example was modern capitalism, which depended on being able to predict and control the processes of production. Understanding mechanical procedures, overseeing workers, employing powerful administrative techniques: all of these were important to the modern capitalist, who must know exactly how much of an item could be produced when. Moreover, intellectualization and rationalization themselves contributed to the process of disenchantment: they acted against belief in magic.

For Weber as for Frazer, magic was the stage of human beliefs and practices before religion. It involved coercing gods in order to satisfy immediate needs: eating, sheltering, avoiding or recovering from disease. It demanded minimal theory and infrastructure. There was no theology or organizing principle governing the divine powers harnessed by magicians; as these divine powers were understood to operate automatically there was no question of having to behave with total moral probity in order to be successful. Perhaps most importantly, there was no continuously existing group comprising practitioners and clients: practitioners were called on by clients each time they were needed. When worshippers collected together into a congregation or 'cult', priests began to replace magicians; the role of priests was distinctly different. Now the magical powers were replaced by a fixed god. Priests were continuously involved in operating the cult, and they established the metaphysics and ethics lacking from magic – a combination that made religion 'rational' in comparison with its more ad hoc predecessor. Members of the religious cult sought less tangible benefits than magicians' clients, such as meaning. It was this that would be stripped away in the last phase of disenchantment, during which science would gain ascendancy and the system of meaning would die with religion. In the meantime, the steady rationalization and removal of magic from religion had culminated in the Protestant Reformation.

Weber's story of this shift from magic to religion was not the whole story: in modern monotheistic societies, magic was still to be found among those social classes where the particular nature of the work and livelihood discouraged further development. Peasants had magical beliefs because their outlook was ineluctably practical, governed by the unpredictable demands of their farming.

Outside Western societies, magic was still to be found; and, according to Weber, its dominance had blocked the rationalization of economic life. 'Magic', he wrote, 'involves a stereotyping of technology and economic relations.' Concerns associated with geomancy had interfered with the construction of railways and factories in China; the Indian caste system made factories unpopular, as it defined too closely what people might do or whom they might have contact with, without falling into a lower caste. 'Obviously, capitalism could not develop', Weber concluded, 'in an economic group thus bound hand and foot by magical beliefs.'

For such benighted groups, hamstrung by a persistent belief in magic, Tylor offered reform. This, for him, was the very purpose of anthropology. Ethnography was about 'aiding progress and removing hindrance'. Identifying the natural laws of the evolution of culture would make it possible to expose 'the remains of crude old culture which have passed into harmful superstition, and to mark these out for destruction'. These remains, and magic was a fine example, were what he called 'survivals': practices or ideas that persisted from earlier periods of a society's development. The 'magical arts' represented 'one of the most pernicious delusions' to which mankind had ever fallen pray, and Tylor condemned 'the whole monstrous farrago'. They were to be overturned by science.

Private rites and powerlessness

Some anthropologists disagreed fundamentally with the assumption that magic belonged in a particular period of a society's development. Tylor, Frazer, and Weber had put forward developmental theories; they had claimed that magic was being (or should be) removed from the world. In contrast, Emile Durkheim (1858–1917), Marcel Mauss (1872–1950), Henri Hubert (1872–1927), Bronislaw Malinowski (1884–1942), and Sir Edward Evan Evans-Pritchard (1902–73) all presented magic, science, and religion not as successive stages but as different aspects of community life. As Malinowski pointed out, people who practise magic do not *only* interact with the world in a magical way.

However, even the difference between religion and magic was a vexed question. Frazer had defined religion as 'a propitiation or conciliation of powers superior to man which are believed to direct and control the course of nature and of human life'. It had a theoretical aspect (believing in higher powers, such as gods) and a practical dimension (doing things to please them). According to Frazer, in a religious regime, nature was considered variable rather than constant, tricky to control and open to interference by those 'higher powers'. It was important to keep the higher powers happy so that they would help by keeping nature in check. Magic was about cause and effect; it assumed that nature was regular and controllable. Frazer acknowledged that magic 'often deals with spirits', but claimed that magicians treated spirits 'in the same fashion' as inanimate objects: it constrained or coerced them. It assumed that they were 'subject to the impersonal forces which control all things'. In short, magicians simply forced spirits to do their bidding. Frazer's account has had many critics. As Stanley Tambiah (b. 1929) has pointed out, to coerce someone is not to treat them as inanimate. It is also worth noting, with Tambiah, that this sounds very like the Protestant critique of Catholicism outlined in chapter 1: a speech that implores is a prayer and is religious; a speech that commands is a spell and is magical.

For Emile Durkheim, the French pioneer of sociology, what distinguished magic from religion was not the nature of the beliefs but the number of people who took part. Magic was a fundamentally individual pursuit, while religion was fundamentally social. Religion, Durkheim claimed, provided a uniting principle that could explain social cohesion. He was suspicious of theories such as Frazer's, which reduced everything to individual psychology; something further was needed, he believed, something that people had in common: values or commitments. Religion united all the members of a society into a 'church' – a single community involving both those who officiated in acts of worship (priests) and others (laity) who did not. Religious acts prompted communal emotional experiences. The practitioner of magic, however, was generally 'a recluse'; even when 'societies of magicians' were formed, these were groups including only the practitioners, not the 'users' of magic whose requests or demands prompted them to act in the first place. Above all, religious rites derived their power precisely from the existence of a community to whom they meant something; magic enjoyed no comparable community.

Nonetheless, Durkheim believed that magic was linked to religion through their use of sacred objects. He divided physical items into two groups: the 'sacred' and the 'profane'. Sacred items were treated with reverence and care, described in beliefs and hedged about with rules of conduct (rites). Religion consisted in these beliefs and rites. The rites had moral force; someone who mishandled a sacred object committed a sin. Magic often dealt with sacred things, but it dealt with them in an entirely profane manner. Although in magic objects were handled according to rules, those rules were practical rather than religious. They reflected the objects' inherent properties. To ignore rules of conduct associated with poisons (for instance) was to risk physical danger, not moral indignation. In Durkheim's system, magic was the practical, non-religious manipulation of religious items, carried out in secret.

As Durkheim's nephew Marcel Mauss and Henri Hubert explained, this distinction on the basis of individual or community focus presented a serious problem. If religion was essentially a social phenomenon deriving its power from the community, then where does magic (by definition lacking such a community) get its power from? The proposal put forward by Mauss and Hubert was that magic *was* social, but in a sense distinct from Durkheim's: practices could only be magical if the whole society believed in their efficacy. Magic was privately practised, but publicly trusted or feared. This distinguished magic from religion: magical rites *did* things – their supposed efficacy was the capacity to produce practical results.

Furthermore, for Mauss and Hubert, magic revealed the existence of a fundamental category which they struggled to describe as a force, a state of being, and an action (among other terms). Originally a Melanesian concept, this was *mana*. It was the medium for magical action and the source of magical power. It was possessed by people and things, and it pervaded the whole world. Sometimes it was mediated by spirits. It explained the powers attributed to particular individuals and magic's supposed action at a distance. In later years, Mauss placed increasing emphasis on *mana* as a fundamental category of which religion and magic were only partially separable expressions ('magico-religious phenomena' now became his term of choice). Even the notion of the 'sacred' could be derived from *mana*. Different

MAUSS, *MANA* AND *ORENDA*

Marcel Mauss provided several examples of the relationship between *mana* and magic. *Mana* was a Melanesian notion, but Mauss identified similar concepts elsewhere. For instance, drawing on earlier work analysing the beliefs of the Huron (an Iroquoian tribe in North America), Mauss explained the notion of *orenda*. Like *mana*, *orenda* was a mysterious, manipulable power with which people and animals, spirits and gods were endowed. Spirits threw their *orenda* up as clouds, where it gave rise to storms; animals' *orenda* conflicted with hunters' to determine the victor in a hunt. *Orenda* was sound – the noises made by animals and rustling plants, the chanting of magicians. In its original sense, the word referred to 'prayers and chants'; all ritual was *orenda*, but it was primarily the power of the shaman, the *raneñdiowa'ne*, someone of powerful *orenda*. A diviner, a *ratreñ'dats* or *hatreñ-dotha*, discovered the future by exhaling or exuding *orenda*. Crucially for Mauss, *orenda* was at magic's heart, particularly 'black magic', possessing practitioners, giving power to spells, amulets, and charms. 'All magic', Mauss explained, 'derives from *orenda*.' However, all ritual was *orenda*, and this provided strong evidence for Mauss that *mana* (or *orenda*) was a more fundamental category than the sacred.

things were *mana* to different degrees, and those that were most *mana* could be considered 'sacred', religious 'in the strict sense'. *Mana* tied magic and religion together in the sacred item; they were distinguished again by the practices applied to the object and the involvement (or not) of the community.

Where Durkheim, Mauss, and Hubert had magic as profane practices with sacred items, Bronislaw Malinowski classified magic itself as sacred. Malinowski, whose work was based on fieldwork carried out in the Trobriand Islands at the eastern end of Papua, had quite different notions of what the categories 'sacred' and 'profane' meant. Sacred activities in this theory were traditional, regarded as sacred by the natives and carried out reverently. Profane activities were practical activities, such as food-gathering or producing items by craft; they were based on observing the world and believing that it would remain the same. The archetypal profane activity (and one in which all societies participated) was science, understood as a set of rules and ideas derived from experience, 'embodied in material achievements' and traditionally carried out by a social organization. Sacred activities included, for instance, all ways of thinking and acting that counted as religion and magic. Like Durkheim, Malinowski thought that religion was a way for groups to reaffirm their social cohesion; where a death wrenched apart social ties, the whole community's participation in funeral rites served to bind people together again. However, religion's place in the community was not its only role – or even the primary one: it also placed each person within the cosmos, explaining origins and destinies; it provided a way of overcoming the fear and experiences of death and misfortune. A religious activity had no aim, no external purpose or goal. Religious ritual was expressive; it allowed participants to articulate their feelings about events such as birth and death.

Magic, in contrast, had practical goals. It was allied to religion rather than science, with rituals, but those rituals were directed towards immediate practical results. Malinowski contrasted initiation rites, which he described as religious because they inculcated particular values, against childbirth rites, which were magical because they were directed towards the safe delivery of children. However, although magical rites were to bring about practical results, they also (like their religious equivalents) had psychological effects that were central to their success: they caused changes in the participants, affecting for instance their hopes and expectations. Like religion, magic was expressive.

For Malinowski, a magical act had three elements: what was said (the formula), what was done (the rite), and the particular state of the performer. During the act, emotion was expressed dramatically using gestures, and items or materials were given powers (through the formula and the rite). Most importantly, the spell itself was powerful because of the phonetic effects in its words, the statements and commands that it contained, its references to myths and ancestors, and the verbal anticipation of its desired effects. Trobrianders, Malinowski wrote, distinguished between the language of magic and that of ordinary speech. Magical speech was different because the words themselves were set apart from those of ordinary language, some meaningless, all treated as sacred, and exercising a special influence; the islanders believed it to be powerful because they saw the world as full of sympathies and forces to be dealt with, and because they understood magical speech to be 'of primeval origin' and to take the form of a 'verbal missile'. Magical speech was, quite simply, odder; it involved unusual and archaic words and grammatical forms; it used metaphor and myth in ways that the ethnographer had to unpick carefully. For Malinowski, this preoccupation with myth, and with overcoming risks and managing luck, placed magic alongside religion rather than as a precursor to science.

Magic's relationship with science was equally clear: magic was what one did when one ran out of science. For Malinowski, a group turned to magic not because they had a pre-religious, pre-scientific mentality, but because they had encountered a situation that they were otherwise powerless to deal with. When magic was used, it was a signal that those employing it had reached the limits of their control over the world; it was directed towards the uncontrollable forces or agencies that affected the outcome of practical activities. Fishing on the Trobriand islands, for instance, would (at least) be begun and ended with magical rites, and building a canoe was a process that demanded a great deal of magical activity, alternating magical procedures with stages of construction. This was believed essential not only to impart greater speed, but because any canoe built without magic

MALINOWSKI AND THE CONSTRUCTION OF A TROBRIAND CANOE

Malinowski discussed Trobrianders' use of magic while making canoes (*Argonauts of the Western Pacific*, 1922); they performed spells and rites at various stages, using special herbs and magical formulas. He provided a translation of a blessing recited over an adze (*ligogu*) used to hollow out the canoe (after saying several untranslatable 'magic' words):

> I shall take hold of an adze, I shall strike! I shall enter my canoe, I shall make thee fly, O canoe, I shall make thee jump! We shall fly like butterflies, like wind; we shall disappear in mist, we shall vanish. You will pierce the straits of Kadimwatu, you will break the promontory of Saramwa, pierce the passage of Loma, die away in the distance, die away with the wind, fade away with the mist, vanish away. Break through your seaweeds [on the shore]. Put on your wreath [i.e. seaweeds?], make your bed in the sand ... Bind your grass skirt together, O canoe [canoe's name], fly!

The reference, Malinowski explained, was to a local myth of a flying canoe, and it was even believed that this might be a physical possibility, had not the necessary spells been lost.

would surely be unseaworthy and unlucky. The fabrication of the vessel itself was still an activity demanding practical skill and care – a badly made canoe would be as unseaworthy as one prepared without magic – but the craftsmanship was necessarily attended with rituals, and differences in how well canoes performed could be attributed to the relative success of those rites.

Malinowski's student Edward Evans-Pritchard concentrated even harder on magical practices – and even less on magical thinking. Durkheim, Mauss, Hubert, and Malinowski had moved away from the approach of Tylor and Frazer, who had seen magic as a mode of thought, a way of understanding the world, a stage in human development; they had replaced this with the notion that magic was a practice to which people occasionally had recourse – something that coexisted with religion and science. Evans-Pritchard, writing on magic in the Sudan, focused on the *function* of magic within the society. He dismissed the approach of trying to work out the underlying rationality of magical acts for the participants (as he noted Tylor, Frazer, and Malinowski had tried to do). For the social anthropologist, he wrote, 'religion is what religion does'. The only genuine way to understand religion was to look at its function in society, not the ideas or beliefs it was supposedly based around, or the structures of thought that it might foster.

Where other anthropologists had begun by distinguishing magic from religion, Evans-Pritchard focused on the difference between 'mystical' and 'empirical' modes of thought. Empirical approaches were those based on experience; mystical 'patterns of thought' dealt in what could not be perceived, or deduced from perceptions. For the Azande, a tribe in north central Africa (mainly in the Congo, the Sudan, and the Central African Republic), the mystical mode provided a way of understanding why particular people fell victim to misfortune. Much of the blame was placed on *mangu*, a substance that was held in the bellies of particular people and projected by them onto victims. To ward off the effects of *mangu*, or to heal illness more generally, the Azande turned to *ngwa*. This word literally meant 'tree' or 'plant', implying a herbal remedy of some kind; in fact animal substances were used too, and spells intoned over them in their preparations. Sometimes *ngwa* could be used to harm people. Evans-Pritchard chose to translate *mangu* as 'witchcraft' and *ngwa* as 'medicine' or 'magic' according to the context in which the word was used; *ngwa* used against people was 'sorcery'. Witchcraft, it is worth noting, is *not* magic in this system; magic is a response to witchcraft. Those who sought a witch responsible for some attack consulted an oracle and relied on divination.

Magic was part of what Evans-Pritchard called a 'ritual complex' – a group of activities involving ritual – whose relationships were key to understanding its constituent parts. Magic, oracles, and witchcraft could not be understood separately; they had to be seen as integrated aspects of a larger system. Magic could not be defined without looking at how it related to oracles and witchcraft, and vice versa. Notwithstanding this reluctance over straightforward defini- tions, Evans-Pritchard did note that magic (good or bad) was carried out in secret, unlike other Zande ritual acts, which were all public. It is possible to recognize here the Durkheim/Mauss notion of magic as private and possibly antisocial versus religion as public. Magic's use as a defence against mystical powers, rather than to affect the physical world directly, meant that Evans-Pritchard did not pursue any comparison with science. The overriding message of his work, however, was that there was no point in trying to formulate universal definitions of terms such as 'magic', or a universal account of the relationship between magic and religion. Frazer and Tylor had been funda- mentally mistaken, but so had Durkheim, Mauss, Huber, and Malinowski.

Magic in modern anthropology

In that way at least, Evans-Pritchard looked to the future of anthropology. The fashion (among anthropologists, at least) for grand theories establishing a dichotomy between magic and religion has largely passed. Even during the productive years of the early anthropologists discussed above, others were rejecting their ideas. R. R. Marett (1866–1943), founder of the Department of Social Anthropology at Oxford, criticized his predecessors for placing too much emphasis on religion as an intellectual exercise at the expense of studying it as an expression of emotion. He agreed broadly that there had been an evolutionary shift from magic towards religion, and adopted a definition of magic that resembled Frazer's and Tylor's; but he denied that the two could be clearly distinguished in the early stages of society, and he used the term 'magico-religious' as a way of combining them.

Alexander Goldenweiser (1880–1940) dismissed Frazer's suggestion that magic was an early form of science, arguing that the two were actually fundamentally different. Frazer had claimed that they both assumed that nature was uniform. According to Goldenweiser, in the case of magic, there was a faith that the same act would provide the same result, but this was based more on an appreciation of the magician's power than anything else. Instead, Goldenweiser linked magic to religion and distinguished them on the basis of whether the attitude concerned was pleading or controlling; he noted nevertheless with Marett that making the distinction was tricky in practice.

W. Lloyd Warner (1898–1970), after living among the Murngin in Australia, rejected Durkheim's theory that magic was by definition pursued in isolation. Warner pointed to his experience of broad community involvement in magic, and specifically in the relationship between the practitioner and the client; there was, in other words, a community for magic that resembled what Durkheim referred to as a 'church'. Magic was no less social than religion.

Fundamentally, all of the theories ran into a similar problem: for any given account of what was magic and what was religion, it was possible to find a group or society whose practices violated it or made it unconvincing. The influential English anthropologist Alfred Radcliffe-Brown (1881–1955) remarked that as there was no agreement over how to define magic and religion or distinguish between them, 'the only sound procedure' was 'to avoid as far as possible the use of the terms in question until there is some general agreement about them'. In the case of magic at least, many anthropologists have followed his suggestion. Many of those who have not incline to a view that does not distinguish as sharply between magic and religion – if at all. Some have made magic a part of religion, others have decided that it is part of a continuum of action that also includes religion; certainly it is seldom now regarded as the intermediate category that it was for earlier anthropologists. Nevertheless, when people are asked to define magic – certainly those outside the discipline of anthropology – it is often to the maxims of Frazer and his successors that they turn. Magic is about manipulating things, religion is about supplicating to gods. It achieves short-term concrete goals rather than long-term diffuse or intangible aims. It is carried out by individuals and may be seen as subversive, where religion functions to support social cohesion. Irrespective of their validity these are tenacious notions.

Anthropology and the history of magic

Anthropological insights have long proved invaluable to historians investigating magic's past in the Western tradition. As organizing principles, guides for investigation or points of debate, those anthropologists who have confronted the issue of how to deal with such beliefs and practices provide inspiration and challenges. Keith Thomas's monumental survey *Religion and the Decline of Magic* (1971) charted the apparent shift away from magical practices in the sixteenth and seventeenth centuries; it provides a key source for much of the material discussed in the first two chapters of this book. It also engaged with Malinowski's theory that magic provided refuge at the limits of people's control over their environment. From a distance this looked convincing, Thomas noted; but people at the end of the seventeenth century had no greater technological influence on the world around them than had their predecessors, yet their belief in magic appeared to have waned. Thomas turned instead to Weber's formulation of the 'disenchantment of the world', and claimed that it was a shift in 'mindset' rather than in material circumstances that had prompted the 'decline of magic' explored by his book. Other historians have been less taken with Weber's theory: the late Robert Scribner detailed the magical beliefs and practices that survived the Reformation and suggested that the idea that the period had seen a drop in 'superstitions' owed more to Weber's observation of nineteenth-century Protestants than it did to any knowledge of the period in question. Scribner concluded his study by remarking that 'I do not think that the thesis about the "disenchantment of the world" will any longer pass muster as a historically accurate description'. Nonetheless, the matter has remained open for historical discussion.

Use of anthropological theories and concepts has, however, also driven historians into the same arguments as anthropologists: how should magic be defined? Is the term useful analytically? The problem is compounded for historians of the Western tradition by the simple fact that they share a common terminology with their historical subjects. People in the past used the word 'magic' themselves, meaning (as we have seen) a variety of different things. Hildred Geertz, an anthropologist, criticized Thomas's book along precisely these lines. Sometimes when Thomas had used the word 'magic', she pointed out, it had been in one of its seventeenth-century senses – recalling that in that period identifying something as magic was a philosophically, theologically, and politically divisive issue. At other times Thomas had used it in a modern sense, more after the fashion of the anthropologists discussed above and perhaps agreeing most strongly with Malinowski's conception (whatever his view of Malinowski's theory). Specifically, Geertz suggested that while Thomas had assumed with Malinowski that magic provided ad hoc responses to immediate practical problems, without any particular theory, in fact magic's underlying principles were not absent but unarticulated. It was not that people simply employed magical procedures without worrying about how they worked or whether they were permissible; rather, they had simply not written down their understandings of these matters for the benefits of nosy historians. Such issues, and the overall question of magic's precise definition, remain critically important to any study: they affect not only the answers a scholar concocts to the research questions, but the choice and framing of those questions in the first place.

Similar issues arose two decades later, when Valerie Flint argued that the early Church had taken on some of the existing pagan practices and beliefs just as it rejected others. They accepted magic where it was strategically important to do so – when strongly espoused by a local community or powerful leader – or when its psychological (or spiritual) effects were desirable. Fellow historian Richard Kieckhefer disagreed. In a review he pointed out that in identifying many of these practices as magical, Flint had directly contradicted the people she was studying. This was not, of course, unintentional: the book's point was precisely to highlight the similarities between those practices rejected as 'magic' by early churchmen and those accepted as legitimate religion. Kieckhefer's point was that the notion of magic as articulated by people in the early Middle Ages had an underlying rationality that did not match that of the notion of magic that Flint herself was importing. Her magic was basically about psychological effects. Theirs was about the intervention of demons or the harnessing of mysterious hidden natural forces. Whether something was to be forbidden depended on whether or not demons must be behind it. Flint, Kieckhefer complained, was contradicting the people she had studied, and in so doing was missing essential attributes of their magic.

Going further back still, we encounter such debates and shifts in the study of ancient periods. Much twentieth-century work on ancient magic paid scant attention to anthropological discussions, focusing on Frazer's if on any (and assuming Frazer's implicitly if not). To such writers, magic was a self-evident category that (like other categories such as 'religion' and 'science') could be used unproblematically to describe other cultures. A curse, an incantation, a divinatory procedure; any of these might without too much consideration be called 'magical'. The awareness by more recent scholars of the significant anthropological literature in the area is exemplified by work such as that of G. E. R. Lloyd.

In his 1979 book *Magic, Reason and Experience*, Lloyd engaged with anthropological work to investigate the relationship between the burgeoning enterprise of philosophy in ancient Greece and the more 'traditional' 'patterns of thought' belonging to 'the complex of phenomena loosely categorized as "magic"'. Under this umbrella he included astrology, alchemy, and 'temple medicine' (in which sufferers would seek divine aid to supply their cures). In an introduction he set out the background in anthropology, footnoting names such as Frazer, Malinowski, and Evans-Pritchard; he described the shift away from treating magic as 'failed applied science' towards understanding it as more about expression than efficacy. Such attitudes as those propounded by Evans-Pritchard and used by Lloyd himself in earlier work were no longer respectable; the easy distinctions between 'mystical', 'common-sense', and 'scientific' ideas now seemed 'simple-minded'. While preparing this groundwork, Lloyd noted that the anthropologist Stanley Tambiah had warned that the history of magic in Europe might not be representative of the whole world – that the shift from 'magic' to 'science' there might be a special case. In fact, as previous scholars had shown, what had happened in ancient Greece was far from a straightforward move from one to the other. Rather, the different approaches to the world had coexisted, and it seemed that magic in later periods actually fed on philosophy, dependent both on its systematic theory and its success. More specifically, Lloyd argued, it was simply not the case that magic was being used by people to cope with situations beyond their control (as Malinowski had proposed). In the case of temple medicine, he reported, the gods were often called on for help in cases that were seen by the ancient Greeks themselves as straightforward – such as injuries caused by simple wounding – as well as for the trickier acute diseases.

In analysing and discussing magic without defining it, *Magic, Reason and Experience* reflected long-standing (and continuing) practices in the study of ancient history; in its engagement with anthropological work it was looking resolutely forward. In the first chapter of a recent book on Mesopotamian magic, Wim van Binsbergen and Frans Wiggermann advocate a similar approach: they draw on the anthropological literature but use the category itself in something akin to a 'common-sense' fashion. The word 'magic', they point out, has not only been in constant use for two thousand years, but came into being specifically in reference to people in that geographical area; Mesopotamian magic was, they explain 'one of the few *original* forms of magic as recognized in the European tradition'. Their explanation of magic draws on Frazer's idea that it involves coercion or constraint, treating natural and spiritual entities alike as subject to mechanistic laws.

As I hope to have shown in this chapter, and in the book as a whole, identifying magic is not so straightforward. The Greek word was an expression of mistrust, not an analytical term; whether or not a medieval charm was magical was a matter of perspective, and what it might mean for something to be called 'magic' varied according to who one asked. Nor did the Greeks mean by magic what medieval writers meant, still less what people mean when they use the term today – whether that be to describe occultism, stage illusion, or some sort of generalized pre-scientific mentality. The tradition that this book has followed has not been a constant, coherent practice given different explanations over the centuries; the activities that might be called magical have changed repeatedly too. For that reason, this book has concentrated as much on the debates surrounding magic as on magical practices themselves, because the debates often defined the subject – not vice versa.

As a result, we have moved a long way from the Persian *magoi* who had excited Greek fears and given rise to the word in the first place. The religious activities that we can ascribe to them were scarcely magical in any modern sense. They were not actually magical in the classical sense either: far from casting spells to control or harm others, they performed sacrifices to the gods and took part in court administration. As far as anthropologists' theories go, the *magoi* took part in their community's rituals rather than private rites; we have no evidence that they put sacred items to profane uses for practical benefit, nor that they held their sacrifices to bind the gods rather than to propitiate them. The magi may have been the origin of the word 'magic', but we can hardly say that they practised it. Magic began as a suspicion, an attitude rather than an act. Small wonder if for many it remains an impression in search of a concept.

Epilogue:
Magic today

What is magic today? People in previous centuries had far clearer pictures of magic and its place in the world than we do. (They disagreed with each other, of course, but they were clear in their disagreements.) Some of the things once practised as magic are little known now; others are no longer considered magical. It has become harder to pinpoint. As Alfred Gell, an anthropologist, put it: magic 'has not disappeared, but has become more diverse and difficult to identify'. So what is magic's place (or places) in the modern world?

There are many possible answers to this question, from cinema to science and from propaganda to paganism. Perhaps the one that comes most readily to mind is stage magic: mention the word 'magic' to most people and they will think of conjuring tricks. However, while illusionism grew out of the magical tradition, the connection is now a distant one. The modern stage magician is an entertainer and magical performances are fakery. Our enjoyment of magic shows is to a great extent predicated on honesty about this artifice: we may not know how tricks are done – in fact, we *should* not know – but we are wholly aware that we are being deceived. The magic is 'not real'. Consider the difference it would make to an audience's reaction if its members genuinely believed that the magician's assistant had been sawn in half and reconnected. Modern conjurors are rationalists, inclined if anything to work against the magical tradition and to direct their expertise towards 'debunking' people who claim paranormal powers or occult wisdom.

If the stage magician is a familiar (if distant) descendant of the European magical tradition, his apparatus has found its way to the heart of modern Western life. Cinema and television arose directly out of the spectacular apparatus of nineteenth-century illusionism, and connect still further back to the wonder-making machinery of previous centuries. They generate the illusion of movement, and present images of things that are not really there. By watching them we can jump through space, switching viewpoints mid-scene, or moving from one country or continent to another in the blink of an eye. In fact, as Erik Barnouw has remarked, it is hardly surprising that early viewers regarded the cinema as magic. What is surprising is that we do not. We treat it as real; we have learned to ignore its illusion. Yet, we do not believe that the things it shows us are actually in the room with us, either. We are aware that cinema and television present things to us that happened somewhere else, some time ago (if at all); what has gone is the wonder. Television and cinema are products of the magical tradition, but they are not magic.

The same has been said of science. Perhaps modern science is magic's offspring; perhaps there is truth in the suggestion that science inherited from magic a desire to experiment and test rather than to contemplate. If there is (and that is far from certain), it is still not the whole story. The situation is too complex to hail magic as science's progenitor. Still, today's science has resonances with Renaissance magic. It is about securing power over nature. It deals with entities and qualities that Renaissance philosophers might well have called 'occult'. Despite the rhetoric of public knowledge, it is practised behind closed doors. Of course, the comparison should not be pushed too far: magic in the Renaissance, as in other periods, was defined against the mainstream. Natural magic examined the phenomena that natural philosophy sidelined. Modern scientific practices are too well respected, established, and accepted to resemble natural magic closely.

Yet more intriguing answers to our question are presented by people who look not for connections to magic's past, but for modern phenomena that fit a definition. They rephrase the question as: what plays the role in modern society that magic has in previous periods (or elsewhere)? As far as Bronislaw Malinowski was concerned, the modern Western manifestation of magic is advertising. Adverts and 'political oratory' involve (like magic) 'sacred' language, 'modern verbal magic'. Advertising copy repeats particular words to produce a reality, from the beauty product that will make its user irresistible, to political propaganda that will convince hearers that 'something really great has been achieved'. Malinowski's modern magic was the art of persuasion that made the unreal real – or, at any rate, made it *seem* so.

To advertisers we can add science-fiction writers. Alfred Gell (1945–97) pointed to these and to 'idealized popular science' writers, calling them the 'propagandists, image-makers and ideologues of technological culture'. These, he wrote, 'are its magicians'. Malinowski had suggested that magic started where technological capability ended; Gell proposed that magic (in its expression of hopes and desires) gave technology something to aim for. In their accounts of what the future held, science-fiction writers were providing magical glimpses of a technological future.

All of this theorising ignores magic's persistence in one obvious form: magic. It is practised by people across the world, in forms recognizable from the nineteenth and twentieth centuries and containing elements far older. It takes place in groups such as covens, or orders owing their existence to the Golden Dawn, and all points in between. According to Tanya Luhrmann, an anthropologist who took part in magical rituals for a period in the 1980s, modern magic is seen by its adherents as a 'mystery religion' centred on some inexpressible hidden (esoteric) knowledge, to be experienced rather than communicated. It is frequently described as a way of achieving self-knowledge; that self-knowledge is believed to allow the practitioner to control the physical world. Luhrmann explained the procedures that practitioners used to keep their ritual lives separate from their everyday existence: secret names, meeting in a special room, wearing robes.

Practitioners believe in magic as a real force in the world. There is some acknowledgement that magic has an expressive, 'symbolic' role in the way it helps people express desires, but Ron Hutton has noted that participants nevertheless believe in magic as a force that is causally effective – if not totally reliable. Luhrmann observed ritual participants entering meditative states and visualizing the desired outcome of their magic. Hutton identifies two broad types of magical operation: magic performed on request, where the practitioner has little investment in the result, and pays slight attention to the outcome, and magic carried out for reasons personally important to the participants. In this second case, the magic is generally used to further a natural process or tip evenly balanced odds towards the desired eventuality. It is used less often where the desired goal is highly unlikely or when it would run against the natural course of events. He also reports a belief in a 'law of threefold return', which claims that magic affects the practitioner just as it does the subject or target; this means that magical acts carried out with evil intent bear 'some kind of psychic penalty' for the person carrying them out, which in turn means that they are too risky to attempt except in dire circumstances.

Above all, magic is about irrationality – for its proponents just as much as its critics. For participants, it is about the search for something *beyond* rationality. The energies that pervade the universe can be detected and influenced by non-rational means – through feelings and dreams, for instance. Rituals involve bypassing the 'rational mind' in order to access these impressions and produce physical effects. None of this signals that practitioners are irrational, still less pre- or sub-rational. Tylor was wrong. Belief in magic does not indicate a more 'primitive' rationality. The intellectual credentials of the subjects of recent studies have been impeccable; practitioners of magic represent most middle-class occupations and professions, with a strong emphasis on IT. Some propose explanations for their magic in terms of modern physics. They cannot be dismissed out of hand as unscientifically minded or caricatured as unable to think rationally. Nor is it obvious that magic is incompatible with the structures and attitudes of contemporary society – though this too has often been suggested.

Magic has largely been defined in opposition to prevailing attitudes: in medieval Christendom, it was unchristian; among Renaissance philosophers, it was practical; in the modern world, it is irrational. This did not stop Christians from practising it and remaining Christians, nor philosophers from participating and persisting with their lofty scholarship. It does not stop people of exemplary rational acuity from taking part. Yet for many this seems surprising, a lapse of judgement or a curious 'survival' of traditional activities. Magic remains a challenge to the comfortable notions of modernity that we have inherited.

Further reading

Introduction: Magic and the magi

Graf, F. 1997. *Magic in the Ancient World*, trans. F. Philip. Cambridge, MA, Harvard University Press

Buhler, S. M. 1990. 'Marsilio Ficino's *De stella magorum* and Renaissance views of the magi.' *Renaissance Quarterly* 43: 348–71

Powell, M. A. 2000. 'The magi as wise men: re-examining a basic supposition.' *New Testament Studies* 46: 1–20

Powell, M. A. 2000. 'The magi as kings: an adventure in reader-response criticism.' *Catholic Biblical Quarterly* 62: 459–80

Chapter 1: A pact with Hell

Bailey, M. D. 2001. 'From sorcery to witchcraft: clerical conceptions of magic in the later Middle Ages.' *Speculum* 76: 960–90

Clark, S. 1997. *Thinking with Demons: the Idea of Witchcraft in Early Modern Europe*. Oxford, Oxford University Press

Kieckhefer, R. 1990. *Magic in the Middle Ages*. Cambridge, Cambridge University Press

Kieckhefer, R. 1997. *Forbidden Rites: A Necromancer's Manual of the Fifteenth Century*. Stroud, Sutton

Scribner, R. W. 1993. 'The Reformation, popular magic, and the "disenchantment of the world".' *Journal of Interdisciplinary History* 23: 475–94

Thorndike, L. 1923–58. *A History of Magic and Experimental Science*. New York, Columbia University Press

Chapter 2: Harnessing nature's hidden powers

Clulee, N. H. 1988. *John Dee's Natural Philosophy: Between Science and Religion*. London, Routledge

Copenhaver, B. P. 1988. 'Astrology and magic.' In Q. Skinner and E. Kesller, eds., *The Cambridge History of Renaissance Philosophy*, 264–300. Cambridge, Cambridge University Press

Copenhaver, B. P. 1998. 'The occultist tradition and its critics.' In D. Garber and M. Ayers, eds, *The Cambridge History of Seventeenth-Century Philosophy*, 454–512. Cambridge, Cambridge University Press

Henry, J. 1986. 'Occult qualities and the experimental philosophy: active principles in pre-Newtonian matter theory.' *History of Science* 24: 335–81

Kassell, L. 2005. *Medicine and Magic in Elizabethan London: Simon Forman: Astrologer, Alchemist, and Physician*. Oxford, Clarendon

Thomas, K. 1971. *Religion and the Decline of Magic: Studies in Popular Beliefs in Sixteenth and Seventeenth Century England*. London, Weidenfeld & Nicolson

Walker, D. P. 1958. *Spiritual and Demonic Magic from Ficino to Campanella*. London, Warburg Institute, University of London

Chapter 3: Tricks and illusions

Barnouw, E. 1981. *The Magician and the Cinema*. New York, Oxford University Press

Butterworth, P. 2005. *Magic on the Early English Stage*. Cambridge, Cambridge University Press

During, S. 2002. *Modern Enchantments: The Cultural Power of Secular Magic*. Cambridge, MA, Harvard University Press

Grafton, A. 2005. *Magic and Technology in Early Modern Europe*. Washington, DC, Smithsonian Institution Libraries. Available at www.sil.si.edu/silpublications/dibner-library-lectures/2002-Grafton/Grafton_2002.pdf

Lamont, P. 2004. *The Rise of the Indian Rope Trick: How Spectacular Hoax Became History*. London, Abacus

Schmidt, L. E. 1998. 'From demon possession to magic show: ventriloquism, religion, and the Enlightenment.' *Church History* 67: 274–304

Chapter 4: The occult

Hutton, R. 1999. *The Triumph of the Moon: a History of Modern Pagan Witchcraft*. Oxford, Oxford University Press

Owne, A. 2004. *The Place of Enchantment: British Occultism and the Culture of the Modern*. Chicago, University of Chicago Press

Katz, D. S. 2005. *The Occult Tradition from the Renaissance to the Present Day*. London, Jonathan Cape

Chapter 5: Analysing magic

Geertz, H. 1975. 'An anthropology of religion and magic, I.' *Journal of Interdisciplinary History* 6: 71–89

Lovejoy, D. S. 1994. 'Satanizing the American Indian.' *The New England Quarterly* 67: 603–21

Tambiah, S. J. 1990. *Magic, Science, Religion, and the Scope of Rationality*. Cambridge, Cambridge University Press

Epilogue: Magic today

Gell, A. 1988. 'Technology and magic.' *Anthropology Today* 4: 6–9

Luhrmann, T. M. 1989. 'The magic of secrecy.' *Ethos* 17: 131–65

Index

Abano, Pietro d' 34
Abbey of Thelema 121
abracadabra 8
Acts of the Apostles xiii, 2, 5
Adamic language 51
advertising 162
Ady, Thomas 71
Africa 133, 134
Agrippa, Heinrich Cornelius
    40, 58, 64, 65, 68, 131;
    *On the Uncertainty and
    Vanity of the Arts and
    Sciences* 53, 66; *Three
    Books of Occult Philosophy*
    40–1, 53–4, 96
Albert the Great 12, 13
alchemy 115–16
'Alexander the Great' 89
Alexandrian Wicca 128
Algeria 135
Allen, Thomas 67
Alpha and Omega 108
Amazing Randi 91–2
Ammianus Marcellinus 5
amulets 6–11, 12
Ancient and Accepted Rite 95
Anderson, John Henry 80, 83
angelic language 51
angels, 21; and magi 49–52
animal magnetism 98–9
animism 137
anthropology 128–9, 130,

135–44; history of magic
    154–9; modern 153–4
Apollonius of Tyana 99
Aquinas, Thomas 12, 13–14,
    33, 37, 49
Archytas 65
Aristotle 61
Arnald of Villanova 15
ars notoria 21, *22*, 51
Ashmole, Elias: *Theatrum
    Chemicum Britannicum* 52
astral light 98–9, 109–14, 118
astral magic 34–7
astral projection 112
astral travel 112
astrology 10, 13–14, 16
Astrum Argentum 118
Atherton, Alexander 47
Aubrey, John 64, 66–7
Augustine of Hippo, St xiii,
    3–4, 9, 11–12, 15
Azande, the 151–2

Bacon, Francis 61
Bacon, Roger xiv, 14, 67
Bale, John 29–30
Bamberg family 80
Baphomet *see* Crowley, Aleister
Baphomet of the Templars
    101, 102, 112, 115
Barbaro, Ermolao 45

Barckseale, William 48
Barnum, P. T. 83
Baronio, Cesare 59
Barrett, Francis: *The Magus, or Celestial Intelligencer* 96
Beast 666, the see Crowley, Aleister
Beck, Martin 82
Benedict XII, pope 20–1
Bennett, Allan 116
Bergson, Mina 105
Bernard of Clairvaux, St 71
Besant, Annie 110
Betson, Thomas 72
Binsbergen, Wim van 158–9
Bishop, Washington Irving 85–6
Blaine, David 91, 92–3
Bland, Edith 105
Blavatsky, H. P. 87, 104, 105
Blue Star Wicca 128
Bodenham, Anne 48
Booker, Robert 46
Bostius, Arnold 53
Bovelles, Charles de 53
Boxley Abbey, Kent 66
Boyle, Robert 52
Brandon, juggler 76
Bromyard, John 9, 12
Brown, Derren 92
Burke, Edward 26
Butler, Samuel 54

cabbala, the 37–9, 100, 105–6, 109, 112–14, 124, 132
Cafres 134
Calvin, John 27, 28, 29
Calvinism 30

Campanella, Tommaso 46
Casaubon, Isaac 59–60
Cathars, the 95–6
Chaldaeans xii
Charles IV, emperor 71
Charles V, emperor 69–70
Charles V of France 10, 71
Charleton, Walter 67, 68
charms 6–11, 12–13, 139–40
Chaucer, Geoffrey: *Canterbury Tales* 44; *Franklin's Tale* 70
Chettle, Henry: *Kind-harts Dream* 72
China 134–5
Choronzon 119–20
Chrétien de Troyes 68
Christ xi–xiii
Christianity 3–4; the Mass 28–30; and pagan charms 8–11; the Reformation 27–31, 143
Church of Aphrodite 123
Church of the Universal Bond 123
Cicero xi
cinema 90–1, 161
Cinématograph 88, 89
clairvoyance 110, 111–12
Clan of the Tubal Cain 127–8
Cobham, Eleanor 47
Cochrane, Robert 128
Committee for Scientific Investigation of Claims of the Paranormal 92
Comus 77–8
conjuror, use of term 64
Constant, Alphonse Louis see Lévi, Éliphas

Constantine I the Great xiv
Cooke, George Alfred 81, 84
Court de Gébelin, Antoine
    100–2
courtly magic 68–71
Crandon, Mina 84
Crinito, Pietro: *De Honesta
    Disciplina* 45
Crowley, Aleister 116–22,
    123–5; *Book of the Law*
    117, 118, 121
cunning men 44–8
curses 2

Davenport, Ira and William
    83, 84
'decollation of John the Baptist'
    trick 74–5
Dee, John 47, 49–51, 55, 65,
    109, 111, 119
Defoe, Daniel: *A Journal of the
    Plague Year* 8
Del Rio, Martin 30
Della Porta, Giambattista 34,
    131; *Magia Naturalis* 41–2
demons 3, 8, 11, 18; *ars notoria*
    21, *22*; and ensnarement
    15–16; and necromancy
    17–20; and talismans
    12–13; and witchcraft 24
Descartes, René 62
Devant, David 81, 88
Dianic Wicca 128
disenchantment of the world
    142, 155
divination 16–22
Doyle, Arthur Conan 84
Drake, Francis 133

During, Simon ix, 86
Durkheim, Emile 144, 145–6,
    148, 151, 152, 153–4

Edison, Thomas 88
Egypt 131–2
Egyptian Hall, London 88
Elymas, the magos xiii, xiv
Emerald Tablet 57–8, 131
empirical modes of thought
    151–2
Enlightenment 78
Enoch 110
Enochian magic 110, 119
Étaples, Jacques Lefevre d' 53,
    57
Evans-Pritchard, Edward 144,
    151–2, 157–8
Evola, Julius 122
Eymeric, Nicholas 23

fascism 122
Father C.R.C. 95
Fawkes, Isaac 76–7
Fay, Anna Eva 85
Feats, Bornelio 75
Ficino, Marsilio xiv, 39, 48–9,
    58, 131; *De Vita Coelitus
    Comparanda* 35–7; healing
    44–5
Flint, Valerie 156–7
Fludd, Robert 65
Folk-Lore Society 126
Forman, Simon 47, 49, 51
Frances, countess of Essex 47
Francini, Tommaso 69
Frater L.E.T. 107

Fraternity of the Rose Cross *see* Rosicrucians
Frazer, James 135–6, 137–42, 144–5, 151, 153, 154, 157, 158–9; Hindu jaundice cure 138
freemasonry 94–6
French, John 53–4
Fuller, John Frederick Charles 118

Gardner, Frederick Leigh 110–11
Gardner, Gerald 27, 123–7; 'Book of Shadows' 124, 125; *Witchcraft Today* 126; 'Ye Bok of ye Art Magical' 124–5
Geertz, Hildred 156
Gell, Alfred 160, 162
geomancy 143
Gerson, Jean 14
Giovio, Paolo 54
Gnosticism 95–6
Goat of Mendes 101, 102
Godfrey of Boulogne 71
Golden Dawn 103–8, 125, 132, 162; magical practice 109–16
Goldenweiser, Alexander 153
gravity 62–3
Great Wizard of the North 80
Gruppo di Ur 122
Gui, Bernard 23
Gypsies 131–2

Hardeen, Theodore 89

Harvey, Gabriel 54
healing 42–3, 44–7
Hebrew language 38–9, 100, 114
Heerbrand, Jacob 28
Helios 4
Henning, Doug 91
Henri IV of France 69
Henry VIII of England 76
Heraclitus xi
heresy 23–4, 30
Hermann family 79–80
Hermes Trismegistus xiv, 57–60, 61, 131
Hermetic corpus 57–60, 61
Hermetic Order of the Golden Dawn *see* Golden Dawn
Hermetic Society 104
Hermetic Society of the M. R. 108
Hermeticism 104, 109
Herodotus xi, xii
Hertz, Carl 89
Hesiod 3
Heth, Joice 83
Hindu jaundice cure 138
Hirsig, Leah 121
Hocus Pocus *see* Vincent, William
hocus pocus 28–9
Hocus Pocus Ivnior 73, 75
Homeopathic Magic 138–9
Homer: *Odyssey* 17
Horniman, Annie 105, 110
Hottentots 133
Houdini, Harry 82, 83–4, 90
Hubert, Henri 144, 146–7, 148, 151
Huguenots 30

Hume, David 137
Huron, the 147
Hus, Jan 30
Hutton, Ron 163

Iamblichus 6
Ignatius of Antioch xii–xiii
Imitative Magic 138–9
Independent and Rectified
    order Rosae Rubeae et
    Aureae Crucis 108
India 134–5, 143–4
Indian fakirs 93, 130
Indian rope trick 87
Industrial Light and Magic 90
Innocent VIII, pope 9
Isaiah 60:3 xiii
Isidore of Seville 4, 16

James I, king: *Daemonologie* 69
Jillette, Penn Fraser 92, 93
John Bull 122
John Chrysostom xiii, 7
John XXII, pope 20
Jourdemayne, Marjory 47
jugglers 71–6
Justin Martyr xii

Kellar, Harry 85; *A Magician's
    Tour* 85
Kelley, Edward (Mr Talbot)
    49–51, 110
Key of Solomon 100–2
Khoikhoi 133
Kieckhefer, Richard 156–7
Kinetoscope 88

Kircher, Athanasius 60
Kiterell 46
Knights Templar 95–6, 101,
    102, 120

La Chapelle, Jean-Baptiste de
    79
Labouchère, Henry 86
Lamont, Peter 87
'Lane', magician 76–7
Langdon, Edmund 45
Lasky, Albrecht 50
Law of Contact or Contagion
    139
Law of Similarity 138–9
Law of Thelema 117
Law of threefold return 163
Ledru, Nicolas-Philippe 77–8
Leibniz, Gottfried Wilhelm
    62–3
Lévi, Éliphas 96–103, 104,
    106, 109, 115, 120, 125;
    *Dogme et Rituel de la Haute
    Magie* 97–8, 100–1
Libanius Gallus 39
Lilly, William 48, 52
Little, Robert Wentworth 104
Lloyd, G. E. R.: *Magic, Reason
    and Experience* 157–8
love magic 47
Lucas, George 90
Luhrmann, Tanya 162–3
Lumière, Louis 88, 89
Luther, Martin 27, 28, 29, 30
Lytton, Edward Bulwer 97

Mackenzie, Kenneth 104, 115

magi, the x–xv, 2, 131, 159; communion with angels 49–52; healing 44–7; lost items 47–8; love magic 47

Magic Circle 81, 86; Occult Committee 86–7

magic lantern 79

magical speech 149

magick 121

magoi see magi, the

Malay charm 139–40

Malinowski, Bronislaw 144, 148–51, 152, 155, 156, 157, 158, 162; *Argonauts of the Western Pacific* 150

Malleus Maleficarum 25, 27

mana 147–8

mangu 151–2

Marett, R. R. 153

'Margery', medium 84

Marlowe, Christopher 68; *The Tragical History of Doctor Faustus* 55–6

Mary of Austria 69

Maskelyne, John Nevil 81, 84, 86–7, 130; *The Fraud of Modern Theosophy Exposed: a Brief History of the Greatest Imposture ever Perpetrated under the Cloak of Religion* 87

Mason, Thomas 48

Mass, the 28–30

mathematical magic 65–8

Mathers, Samuel Liddell MacGregor 103–5, 107–8, 109–10, 115, 119; and Crowley 116–17; *The Sacred Magic of Abramelin*

the Mage 117

matter, properties of 61–3

Matthew, Gospel of xi–xiii, xiv

Mauss, Marcel 144, 151, 152

Maximilian I, emperor 69

mechanical philosophy 62

mechanics 65–8

Medici, Cosimo de' 58

Medici, Ferdinand I de' 69

Méliès Kinétograph 89

Méliès, Maris-George-Jean 88–9, 90

mentalist performers 84–7

Mesmer, Anton 98

Mesopotamia 158–9

Michaëlis, Sebastien 30–1

Montaigne, Michel de 69

More, Henry 28

Mosaical rods 48

Moses: and the cabbala 132; and the Pharaoh 3, 4, 15, 131

Munich handbook of necromancy 70

Murray, Margaret 27, 123

mystery religion 162–3

mystical modes of thought 151–2

Napoleon III 135

Nashe, Thomas: *The Unfortunate Traveller* 68

National Laboratory for Psychical Science 86

natural philosophy 33, 60–3

Nazi regime 122

necromancy 17–20, 70, 98

Neoplatonism 5–6, 58

Nesbit, E. 105

Neuburg, Victor 118–20
New Age 127
Newton, Isaac 60, 62–3
ngwa 152
Nider, Johannes 24–5
Nodé, Pierre 30

occultism 97
Odin 4
Order of the Rosy Cross 104
Ordo Rosae Rubeae et Aureae
    Crucis 107
Ordo Templi Orientis 120,
    122, 123–4
orenda 147
Oresme, Nicole 13–15
Origen xii
Orpheus xiv
Overbury, Thomas 47

pagan witchcraft 122–8
Pan 101, 119
Paracelsianism 42–3
Paracelsus 40, 42–3, 54–5
Paul, R. W. 88
pawwaws 132–3
Penn & Teller 92
pentagram 99–100
Pentagrammaton 38–9
Petrarch xiv
phantasmagoria 79
Pharaoh: and Moses 3, 4, 15,
    131
pharmakeia 22
Philadelphia Report 85
Philip, Prince of Spain 69
Philip VI of France 20
Philo of Alexandria x

philosophers' stone 51–2
Picart, Bernard 133, 134
Picatrix 10–11, 17, 19
Pico della Mirandola, Giovanni
    33–5, 37–8, 39, 45, 52,
    57, 58
Pinchbeck, William 82–3
Pinetti, Giovanni Giuseppe 78
Pingree, Annie 85
Plato ix, xiv, 3, 5, 52, 59
Pliny the Elder x, xi; *Natural
    History* 7
Plotinus x, 5–6
Porphyry 6
prayers 12
Price, Harry 86
priests 143
prophets x
Psalm 72, xiii
Ptolemy 16
Puritanism 142
Pythagoras xiv

Rabelais, François 117
Radcliffe-Brown, Alfred 154
Raleigh, Walter 52
Ramsey, Davy 48
Raziel, angel 51
Recorde, Robert 67
Redman, John 47
Reformation, the 27–31, 143
Regiomontanus 69
religion: magic as 144–52,
    153–4
Reuchlin, Johann: *De Verbo
    Mirifico* 38, 39
Reuss, Theodor 120
Rid, Samuel 131–2

Rider-Waite-Smith tarot 115, 125
rising in the planes 112
Robert-Houdin, Jean-Eugène 80–1, 82, 83, 90, 135
Robertson, Étienne Gaspard 79; *Fantasmagorie* 87
Rosencreutz, Christian 95, 107, 132
Rosicrucians 94–6, 104, 132
Rowley, John 66
Royal Society 26
Rudolf II, emperor 50–1

sacraments 29
sacred: magic as 148–9; objects and practices 146–8
Samuel, the prophet 17
Sanders, Alex 128
Sanford, James 54
science 140, 148, 149–51, 161
science fiction 162
Scientific American 84
Scot, Reginald 7, 74–6; *The Discouerie of Witchcraft* 26, 75, 76
Scotto, Girolamo 68–9
screen magic 87–93
Scribner, Robert 155
scrying 111–12
sex magic 120–1
Shakespeare, William: *The Tempest* 56–7
sigils 48–9
signatures, doctrine of 43
Simon Magus xiii, xiv, 2, 5, 30
Simos, Miriam *see* Starhawk
Slade, Henry 85

Societas Rosicruciana 104, 105
Society of American Magicians 81, 82
Socrates 3
soliloquia 38
Solomon 21, 51
soothsayers x
sorcery and sorcerers ix, 6
soul, the: power of 14–15
spells 12–13
spiritualism 83–4
Sprengel, Anna 103
St. George's Hall, London 90
stage magic 76–82, 160
Star Wars 90
Starhawk: *The Spiral Dance* 127
Summers, Montague 27
superstition 13
Swane, Goodwife 47
symbols 115
Sympathetic Magic 139–40

taboo 140
Tacitus xi
Talbot, Mr *see* Kelley, Edward
talismans 6–11, 12, 37
Tambiah, Stanley 145, 158
tarot 100–2, 111, 114; Rider-Waite-Smith tarot 115, 125
tattvas 111, 115
television 161
Teller, Raymond Joseph 92
temple medicine 157, 158
Tetragrammaton 38
The Magic Circular 81
The Magick of Kirani, King of Persia 42

The Mysteries of Myra 89
Théâtre Robert-Houdin, Paris
    88–9
Theophrast Bombast von
    Hohenheim *see* Paracelsus
Theosophical Society 87, 104,
    105
theurgy 6
Thomas, Keith 156; *Religion
    and the Decline of Magic*
    155
Tillotson, John 28–9
transubstantiation 28
Tree of Life 105–6, 112–14
tregetour 71
Trithemius, Johannes 39–40,
    52–3
Trobriand Islands 148, 149,
    150–1
Truth 86
Turner, Anne 47
Tylor, Edward 135–44, 151,
    163; *Primitive Culture* 136

Uriel, angel 50–1

Veazy, Goodwife 45
ventriloquism 78–9
Victor, Alexander 89
Vincent, William 73, 75
Voltaire xv

Waite, A. E. 96, 108
Walsh, John 48
Warner, W. Lloyd 153–4
Weber, Max 142–4, 155

Weiss, Eric *see* Houdini, Harry
Westcott, William Wynn
    103–5, 106, 107–8
Wicca 126–8
Wiligut, Karl Maria 122
Wilkins, John 68; *Mathematicall
    Magick* 67
William of Auvergne 33
Wilson, Mark 91
witch of Endor 17
witches and witchcraft 22–7,
    30–1, 152; and paganism
    122–8
Woden 4
Woodford, Alphonsus F. A.
    103
Woodman, William Robert
    103
Wyclif, John 30

Xenophon xi

Yarmouth Independent 26
Yates, Frances 58, 60–1
Yates thesis 60–1
Yeats, William Butler 105,
    107, 115, 116

Zarathustra *see* Zoroaster
Zeus 3
Zoroaster xi, xiv, 7
Zoroastrianism xi
Zwinge, Randall James
    Hamilton *see* Amazing
    Randi
Zwingli, Ulrich 27, 28